TEACHER'S PET PUBLICATIONS

PUZZLE PACK
for
Dicey's Song
based on the book by
Cynthia Voigt

Written by
William T. Collins

© 2005 Teacher's Pet Publications
All Rights Reserved

The materials in this packet are copyrighted
by Teacher's Pet Publications, Inc.

These pages may be duplicated by the purchaser
for use in the purchaser's own classroom.

Copying any of these materials and distributing them
for any other purpose is a violation of the copyright laws.

© 2005 Teacher's Pet Publications, Inc.
www.tpet.com

INTRODUCTION
If you already own the LitPlan for this title, this Puzzle Pack will refresh your Unit Resource Materials and Vocabulary Resource Materials sections plus give you additional materials you can substitute into the tests. If you do not already have a complete LitPlan, these pages will give you some supplemental materials to use with your own plan. There are two main groups of materials: one set for unit words (such as characters' names, symbols, places, etc.) and one set for vocabulary words associated with the book.

WORD LIST
There is a word list for both the unit words and the vocabulary words. These lists show you which words are being used in the materials and the clues or definitions being used for those words. You may want to give students a word list with clues/definitions to help them, or you may want students to only have a word list (without clues/definitions) if you want them to work a little harder. Both are available for duplication. The word lists can also be your "calling key" for the bingo games.

FILL IN THE BLANK AND MATCHING
There are 4 each of the fill in the blank and matching worksheets for both the unit and vocabulary words. These pages can be used either as extra worksheets for students or as objective parts of a unit test. They can be done individually if students need extra help or as a whole class activity to review the material covered.

MAGIC SQUARES
The magic squares not only reinforce the material covered but also work on reasoning and math skills. Many teachers have told us that their students really enjoy doing these!

WORD SEARCH PUZZLES
The word search words go in all directions, as indicated on your answer keys. Two of the word search puzzles have the clues listed rather than the words. This makes the puzzle a little more difficult, but it reinforces the material better. Two word search puzzles have words only for students who find the clue puzzles too difficult.

CROSSWORD PUZZLES
Both unit and vocabulary word sections have 4 crossword puzzles.

BINGO CARDS
There are 32 individual bingo cards for the unit words and 32 individual bingo cards for the vocabulary words. You can use your word list as a "call list," calling the words at random and marking them off of your list as you go, or you could use the flash cards by cutting them apart and drawing the words at random from a hat (or box or whatever). To make a better review, you might ask for the definition and spelling of each word as you call it out–or you could call out the definitions and have students tell you the words they need to look for on the puzzle.

JUGGLE LETTERS
The vocabulary juggle letter game is intended to help students learn the spellings of the words. One sheet has the definitions listed on it as an extra help for students who need it or to reinforce the definitions if you choose to do so.

FLASH CARDS
We've included a set of vocabulary flash cards you can duplicate, cut, and fold for your students. Some teachers make a few sets for general use by the class; others make a set for each student. Some teachers duplicate them for each student and have the students cut & fold their own. You can cut out just the words and put them in a hat, have each student pick out one word and write the definition and a sentence for that word. Students then swap words and papers, with the next student adding a sentence of his own under the last one. You can have students swap as many times as you like. Each time the student will read the sentences written prior to his own and then add a sentence. You can cut out the words and definitions separately and play "I Have; Who Has?" Each student in the room draws a word and definition. The first student says, "I have (the name of the word). Who has the definition?" The student with the definition reads it then says, "I have (the name of the vocabulary word she has). Who has the definition?" The round continues until all words and definitions have been given.

Dicey's Song Word List

No.	Word	Clue/Definition
1.	ADOPTION	Process by which Gram became guardian of the children
2.	ANGEL	Dicey says Maybeth looks like a Christmas ____
3.	APRON	Everyone laughed at Dicey's ____; her home-ec creation
4.	ATTIC	The children got into trouble looking at things in Gram's ____
5.	BOAT	Gram's transportation downtown
6.	BOOTLEGGING	Former illegal profession of the Tillermans
7.	BOSTON	City where Momma was staying
8.	BOX	The man at the wood store gave Dicey a ____
9.	CHAPPELLE	English teacher
10.	CRISFIELD	Town where Dicey lives
11.	DICEY	Brings the Tillerman children to Crisfield
12.	ESSAY	Mr. Chappelle accused Dicey of plagiarizing her ____
13.	EVERSLEIGH	Home Ec teacher
14.	FAT	Mr. Lingerle's physical condition
15.	GRAM	Adopted the children
16.	GROCERY	Millie owned a ____ store
17.	GUITAR	Jeff's instrument
18.	HONKY	Mina's friends called Dicey this name
19.	JAMES	Liked to read; Dicey's brother
20.	JEFF	Played guitar after school
21.	JOHN	Gram's husband
22.	LINGERLE	Music teacher
23.	LIZA	Momma
24.	MARBLES	Gram won these from the second graders
25.	MAYBETH	Slow learner; talented musician
26.	MILLIE	Store owner
27.	MINA	Dicey's school friend
28.	MONEY	Mr. Lingerle gave Gram an envelope with ____ in it
29.	MULBERRY	They buried Momma under the paper ____ tree
30.	MUSIC	Maybeth's talent
31.	NOTE	Dicey had one from the music teacher requesting a conference
32.	OCEAN	Dicey's conversations with Mina were 'like running along the ____'
33.	READ	Dicey wanted James to find a way to help Maybeth ____
34.	ROCKET	Dicey bought Sammy a toy ____
35.	SAILBOAT	Dicey's pot of gold
36.	SAMMY	Wanted to help Dicey with the boat
37.	SCIENCE	Dicey and Wilhemina worked together on a ____ project
38.	SEVEN	Sammy's age
39.	SPOON	Gram sells it to get money to go to Boston
40.	TEN	James's age
41.	THIRTEEN	Dicey's age at the beginning of the book
42.	VOIGT	Author
43.	WELFARE	Gram gets these checks

Dicey's Song Fill In The Blanks 1

_____

_____

_____

_____

_____

_____

_____

_____

_____

_____

_____

_____

_____

_____

_____

_____

_____

_____

_____

_____

1. Jeff's instrument
2. Store owner
3. They buried Momma under the paper ____ tree
4. Home Ec teacher
5. Dicey had one from the music teacher requesting a conference
6. Everyone laughed at Dicey's ____; her home-ec creation
7. Dicey's pot of gold
8. Author
9. Dicey's conversations with Mina were 'like running along the ____'
10. Liked to read; Dicey's brother
11. Former illegal profession of the Tillermans
12. The children got into trouble looking at things in Gram's ____
13. Mr. Lingerle gave Gram an envelope with ____ in it
14. Mr. Chappelle accused Dicey of plagiarizing her ____
15. Gram gets these checks
16. Adopted the children
17. Played guitar after school
18. The man at the wood store gave Dicey a ____
19. Mr. Lingerle's physical condition
20. Gram won these from the second graders

Dicey's Song Fill In The Blanks 1 Answer Key

GUITAR	1. Jeff's instrument
MILLIE	2. Store owner
MULBERRY	3. They buried Momma under the paper ____ tree
EVERSLEIGH	4. Home Ec teacher
NOTE	5. Dicey had one from the music teacher requesting a conference
APRON	6. Everyone laughed at Dicey's ____; her home-ec creation
SAILBOAT	7. Dicey's pot of gold
VOIGT	8. Author
OCEAN	9. Dicey's conversations with Mina were 'like running along the ____'
JAMES	10. Liked to read; Dicey's brother
BOOTLEGGING	11. Former illegal profession of the Tillermans
ATTIC	12. The children got into trouble looking at things in Gram's ____
MONEY	13. Mr. Lingerle gave Gram an envelope with ____ in it
ESSAY	14. Mr. Chappelle accused Dicey of plagiarizing her ____
WELFARE	15. Gram gets these checks
GRAM	16. Adopted the children
JEFF	17. Played guitar after school
BOX	18. The man at the wood store gave Dicey a ____
FAT	19. Mr. Lingerle's physical condition
MARBLES	20. Gram won these from the second graders

Dicey's Song Fill In The Blanks 2

_____

1. Adopted the children
2. Momma
3. Dicey says Maybeth looks like a Christmas ____
4. Dicey bought Sammy a toy ____
5. Gram's husband
6. English teacher
7. Dicey's conversations with Mina were 'like running along the ____'
8. Gram gets these checks
9. Gram sells it to get money to go to Boston
10. Dicey's age at the beginning of the book
11. The children got into trouble looking at things in Gram's ____
12. Played guitar after school
13. Brings the Tillerman children to Crisfield
14. Town where Dicey lives
15. Mr. Lingerle gave Gram an envelope with ____ in it
16. Millie owned a ____ store
17. Home Ec teacher
18. They buried Momma under the paper ____ tree
19. Dicey and Wilhemina worked together on a ____ project
20. Jeff's instrument

7
Copyrighted

Dicey's Song Fill In The Blanks 2 Answer Key

GRAM	1. Adopted the children
LIZA	2. Momma
ANGEL	3. Dicey says Maybeth looks like a Christmas ____
ROCKET	4. Dicey bought Sammy a toy ____
JOHN	5. Gram's husband
CHAPPELLE	6. English teacher
OCEAN	7. Dicey's conversations with Mina were 'like running along the ____'
WELFARE	8. Gram gets these checks
SPOON	9. Gram sells it to get money to go to Boston
THIRTEEN	10. Dicey's age at the beginning of the book
ATTIC	11. The children got into trouble looking at things in Gram's ____
JEFF	12. Played guitar after school
DICEY	13. Brings the Tillerman children to Crisfield
CRISFIELD	14. Town where Dicey lives
MONEY	15. Mr. Lingerle gave Gram an envelope with ____ in it
GROCERY	16. Millie owned a ____ store
EVERSLEIGH	17. Home Ec teacher
MULBERRY	18. They buried Momma under the paper ____ tree
SCIENCE	19. Dicey and Wilhemina worked together on a ____ project
GUITAR	20. Jeff's instrument

Dicey's Song Fill In The Blanks 3

_____

_____

_____

_____

_____

_____

_____

_____

_____

_____

_____

_____

_____

_____

_____

_____

_____

_____

_____

_____

1. Wanted to help Dicey with the boat
2. Mr. Lingerle's physical condition
3. Author
4. English teacher
5. Gram's transportation downtown
6. Dicey had one from the music teacher requesting a conference
7. Gram's husband
8. They buried Momma under the paper ____ tree
9. Store owner
10. Everyone laughed at Dicey's ____; her home-ec creation
11. Played guitar after school
12. Dicey's pot of gold
13. Gram sells it to get money to go to Boston
14. Dicey and Wilhemina worked together on a ____ project
15. Mr. Lingerle gave Gram an envelope with ____ in it
16. Millie owned a ____ store
17. Liked to read; Dicey's brother
18. The man at the wood store gave Dicey a ____
19. Home Ec teacher
20. Jeff's instrument

Dicey's Song Fill In The Blanks 3 Answer Key

SAMMY	1. Wanted to help Dicey with the boat
FAT	2. Mr. Lingerle's physical condition
VOIGT	3. Author
CHAPPELLE	4. English teacher
BOAT	5. Gram's transportation downtown
NOTE	6. Dicey had one from the music teacher requesting a conference
JOHN	7. Gram's husband
MULBERRY	8. They buried Momma under the paper ____ tree
MILLIE	9. Store owner
APRON	10. Everyone laughed at Dicey's ____; her home-ec creation
JEFF	11. Played guitar after school
SAILBOAT	12. Dicey's pot of gold
SPOON	13. Gram sells it to get money to go to Boston
SCIENCE	14. Dicey and Wilhemina worked together on a ____ project
MONEY	15. Mr. Lingerle gave Gram an envelope with ____ in it
GROCERY	16. Millie owned a ____ store
JAMES	17. Liked to read; Dicey's brother
BOX	18. The man at the wood store gave Dicey a ____
EVERSLEIGH	19. Home Ec teacher
GUITAR	20. Jeff's instrument

Dicey's Song Fill In The Blanks 4

_____

_____

_____

_____

_____

_____

_____

_____

_____

_____

_____

_____

_____

_____

_____

_____

_____

_____

_____

_____

1. Maybeth's talent
2. Mr. Chappelle accused Dicey of plagiarizing her ____
3. Dicey's school friend
4. Dicey and Wilhemina worked together on a ____ project
5. Music teacher
6. Dicey's conversations with Mina were 'like running along the ____'
7. Dicey's age at the beginning of the book
8. They buried Momma under the paper ____ tree
9. English teacher
10. Millie owned a ____ store
11. The man at the wood store gave Dicey a ____
12. Played guitar after school
13. Dicey says Maybeth looks like a Christmas ____
14. Dicey bought Sammy a toy ____
15. Adopted the children
16. Gram's husband
17. Former illegal profession of the Tillermans
18. The children got into trouble looking at things in Gram's ____
19. Dicey wanted James to find a way to help Maybeth ____
20. Dicey had one from the music teacher requesting a conference

Dicey's Song Fill In The Blanks 4 Answer Key

MUSIC	1. Maybeth's talent
ESSAY	2. Mr. Chappelle accused Dicey of plagiarizing her ____
MINA	3. Dicey's school friend
SCIENCE	4. Dicey and Wilhemina worked together on a ____ project
LINGERLE	5. Music teacher
OCEAN	6. Dicey's conversations with Mina were 'like running along the ____'
THIRTEEN	7. Dicey's age at the beginning of the book
MULBERRY	8. They buried Momma under the paper ____ tree
CHAPPELLE	9. English teacher
GROCERY	10. Millie owned a ____ store
BOX	11. The man at the wood store gave Dicey a ____
JEFF	12. Played guitar after school
ANGEL	13. Dicey says Maybeth looks like a Christmas ____
ROCKET	14. Dicey bought Sammy a toy ____
GRAM	15. Adopted the children
JOHN	16. Gram's husband
BOOTLEGGING	17. Former illegal profession of the Tillermans
ATTIC	18. The children got into trouble looking at things in Gram's ____
READ	19. Dicey wanted James to find a way to help Maybeth ____
NOTE	20. Dicey had one from the music teacher requesting a conference

Dicey's Song Matching 1

___ 1. SAMMY
___ 2. SEVEN
___ 3. ADOPTION
___ 4. JAMES
___ 5. CHAPPELLE
___ 6. ROCKET
___ 7. MINA
___ 8. HONKY
___ 9. JOHN
___10. MARBLES
___11. TEN
___12. SPOON
___13. THIRTEEN
___14. SAILBOAT
___15. MUSIC
___16. BOAT
___17. BOX
___18. READ
___19. MONEY
___20. SCIENCE
___21. ATTIC
___22. OCEAN
___23. EVERSLEIGH
___24. GUITAR
___25. ESSAY

A. Wanted to help Dicey with the boat
B. Dicey's school friend
C. Gram won these from the second graders
D. Gram sells it to get money to go to Boston
E. The man at the wood store gave Dicey a ____
F. Dicey's pot of gold
G. Sammy's age
H. Dicey wanted James to find a way to help Maybeth ____
I. Mina's friends called Dicey this name
J. Maybeth's talent
K. Mr. Chappelle accused Dicey of plagiarizing her ____
L. Jeff's instrument
M. Gram's transportation downtown
N. Dicey bought Sammy a toy ____
O. Liked to read; Dicey's brother
P. Dicey and Wilhemina worked together on a ____ project
Q. Gram's husband
R. English teacher
S. Mr. Lingerle gave Gram an envelope with ____ in it
T. The children got into trouble looking at things in Gram's ____
U. Dicey's age at the beginning of the book
V. Home Ec teacher
W. James's age
X. Process by which Gram became guardian of the children
Y. Dicey's conversations with Mina were 'like running along the ____'

Dicey's Song Matching 1 Answer Key

A - 1. SAMMY		A. Wanted to help Dicey with the boat
G - 2. SEVEN		B. Dicey's school friend
X - 3. ADOPTION		C. Gram won these from the second graders
O - 4. JAMES		D. Gram sells it to get money to go to Boston
R - 5. CHAPPELLE		E. The man at the wood store gave Dicey a ____
N - 6. ROCKET		F. Dicey's pot of gold
B - 7. MINA		G. Sammy's age
I - 8. HONKY		H. Dicey wanted James to find a way to help Maybeth ____
Q - 9. JOHN		I. Mina's friends called Dicey this name
C -10. MARBLES		J. Maybeth's talent
W -11. TEN		K. Mr. Chappelle accused Dicey of plagiarizing her ____
D -12. SPOON		L. Jeff's instrument
U -13. THIRTEEN		M. Gram's transportation downtown
F -14. SAILBOAT		N. Dicey bought Sammy a toy ____
J -15. MUSIC		O. Liked to read; Dicey's brother
M -16. BOAT		P. Dicey and Wilhemina worked together on a ____ project
E -17. BOX		Q. Gram's husband
H -18. READ		R. English teacher
S -19. MONEY		S. Mr. Lingerle gave Gram an envelope with ____ in it
P -20. SCIENCE		T. The children got into trouble looking at things in Gram's ____
T -21. ATTIC		U. Dicey's age at the beginning of the book
Y -22. OCEAN		V. Home Ec teacher
V -23. EVERSLEIGH		W. James's age
L -24. GUITAR		X. Process by which Gram became guardian of the children
K -25. ESSAY		Y. Dicey's conversations with Mina were 'like running along the ____'

Dicey's Song Matching 2

___ 1. ATTIC   A. Mr. Lingerle's physical condition
___ 2. MAYBETH   B. James's age
___ 3. OCEAN   C. Music teacher
___ 4. JEFF   D. Mr. Chappelle accused Dicey of plagiarizing her ____
___ 5. GRAM   E. Process by which Gram became guardian of the children
___ 6. ADOPTION   F. The man at the wood store gave Dicey a ____
___ 7. BOAT   G. English teacher
___ 8. LINGERLE   H. Adopted the children
___ 9. JOHN   I. Gram's husband
___10. MUSIC   J. Played guitar after school
___11. DICEY   K. Gram gets these checks
___12. EVERSLEIGH   L. Momma
___13. ESSAY   M. Maybeth's talent
___14. BOX   N. The children got into trouble looking at things in Gram's ____
___15. THIRTEEN   O. Dicey had one from the music teacher requesting a conference
___16. READ   P. Slow learner; talented musician
___17. TEN   Q. Gram's transportation downtown
___18. CHAPPELLE   R. Dicey's age at the beginning of the book
___19. WELFARE   S. Dicey wanted James to find a way to help Maybeth ____
___20. SEVEN   T. Sammy's age
___21. VOIGT   U. Home Ec teacher
___22. FAT   V. Dicey's conversations with Mina were 'like running along the ____'
___23. LIZA   W. Dicey bought Sammy a toy ____
___24. NOTE   X. Author
___25. ROCKET   Y. Brings the Tillerman children to Crisfield

Dicey's Song Matching 2 Answer Key

N - 1. ATTIC		A. Mr. Lingerle's physical condition
P - 2. MAYBETH		B. James's age
V - 3. OCEAN		C. Music teacher
J - 4. JEFF		D. Mr. Chappelle accused Dicey of plagiarizing her ____
H - 5. GRAM		E. Process by which Gram became guardian of the children
E - 6. ADOPTION		F. The man at the wood store gave Dicey a ____
Q - 7. BOAT		G. English teacher
C - 8. LINGERLE		H. Adopted the children
I - 9. JOHN		I. Gram's husband
M -10. MUSIC		J. Played guitar after school
Y -11. DICEY		K. Gram gets these checks
U -12. EVERSLEIGH		L. Momma
D -13. ESSAY		M. Maybeth's talent
F -14. BOX		N. The children got into trouble looking at things in Gram's ____
R -15. THIRTEEN		O. Dicey had one from the music teacher requesting a conference
S -16. READ		P. Slow learner; talented musician
B -17. TEN		Q. Gram's transportation downtown
G -18. CHAPPELLE		R. Dicey's age at the beginning of the book
K -19. WELFARE		S. Dicey wanted James to find a way to help Maybeth ____
T -20. SEVEN		T. Sammy's age
X -21. VOIGT		U. Home Ec teacher
A -22. FAT		V. Dicey's conversations with Mina were 'like running along the ____'
L -23. LIZA		W. Dicey bought Sammy a toy ____
O -24. NOTE		X. Author
W -25. ROCKET		Y. Brings the Tillerman children to Crisfield

Dicey's Song Matching 3

___ 1. MAYBETH   A. Author
___ 2. MONEY   B. Gram's transportation downtown
___ 3. JAMES   C. Dicey says Maybeth looks like a Christmas ____
___ 4. SPOON   D. Dicey wanted James to find a way to help Maybeth ____
___ 5. ANGEL   E. Process by which Gram became guardian of the children
___ 6. BOAT   F. James's age
___ 7. CHAPPELLE   G. Gram sells it to get money to go to Boston
___ 8. GRAM   H. Maybeth's talent
___ 9. NOTE   I. Momma
___10. HONKY   J. Mina's friends called Dicey this name
___11. MARBLES   K. Slow learner; talented musician
___12. BOX   L. Liked to read; Dicey's brother
___13. MUSIC   M. The man at the wood store gave Dicey a ____
___14. THIRTEEN   N. They buried Momma under the paper ____ tree
___15. VOIGT   O. Former illegal profession of the Tillermans
___16. MULBERRY   P. Dicey's age at the beginning of the book
___17. GROCERY   Q. Dicey had one from the music teacher requesting a conference
___18. TEN   R. English teacher
___19. SAILBOAT   S. Store owner
___20. LIZA   T. Gram's husband
___21. JOHN   U. Gram won these from the second graders
___22. READ   V. Dicey's pot of gold
___23. MILLIE   W. Adopted the children
___24. ADOPTION   X. Millie owned a ____ store
___25. BOOTLEGGING   Y. Mr. Lingerle gave Gram an envelope with ____ in it

Dicey's Song Matching 3 Answer Key

K - 1. MAYBETH		A. Author
Y - 2. MONEY		B. Gram's transportation downtown
L - 3. JAMES		C. Dicey says Maybeth looks like a Christmas ____
G - 4. SPOON		D. Dicey wanted James to find a way to help Maybeth ____
C - 5. ANGEL		E. Process by which Gram became guardian of the children
B - 6. BOAT		F. James's age
R - 7. CHAPPELLE		G. Gram sells it to get money to go to Boston
W - 8. GRAM		H. Maybeth's talent
Q - 9. NOTE		I. Momma
J - 10. HONKY		J. Mina's friends called Dicey this name
U - 11. MARBLES		K. Slow learner; talented musician
M - 12. BOX		L. Liked to read; Dicey's brother
H - 13. MUSIC		M. The man at the wood store gave Dicey a ____
P - 14. THIRTEEN		N. They buried Momma under the paper ____ tree
A - 15. VOIGT		O. Former illegal profession of the Tillermans
N - 16. MULBERRY		P. Dicey's age at the beginning of the book
X - 17. GROCERY		Q. Dicey had one from the music teacher requesting a conference
F - 18. TEN		R. English teacher
V - 19. SAILBOAT		S. Store owner
I - 20. LIZA		T. Gram's husband
T - 21. JOHN		U. Gram won these from the second graders
D - 22. READ		V. Dicey's pot of gold
S - 23. MILLIE		W. Adopted the children
E - 24. ADOPTION		X. Millie owned a ____ store
O - 25. BOOTLEGGING		Y. Mr. Lingerle gave Gram an envelope with ____ in it

Copyrighted

Dicey's Song Matching 4

___ 1. HONKY
___ 2. GUITAR
___ 3. SAMMY
___ 4. MILLIE
___ 5. ROCKET
___ 6. CRISFIELD
___ 7. JAMES
___ 8. MUSIC
___ 9. ADOPTION
___10. BOAT
___11. ANGEL
___12. READ
___13. VOIGT
___14. LINGERLE
___15. GRAM
___16. NOTE
___17. SAILBOAT
___18. JEFF
___19. SPOON
___20. OCEAN
___21. FAT
___22. SCIENCE
___23. MINA
___24. WELFARE
___25. APRON

A. Maybeth's talent
B. Mr. Lingerle's physical condition
C. Dicey's school friend
D. Dicey says Maybeth looks like a Christmas ____
E. Dicey wanted James to find a way to help Maybeth ____
F. Everyone laughed at Dicey's ____; her home-ec creation
G. Process by which Gram became guardian of the children
H. Dicey's conversations with Mina were 'like running along the ____'
I. Gram gets these checks
J. Wanted to help Dicey with the boat
K. Played guitar after school
L. Store owner
M. Jeff's instrument
N. Gram sells it to get money to go to Boston
O. Town where Dicey lives
P. Adopted the children
Q. Author
R. Music teacher
S. Mina's friends called Dicey this name
T. Gram's transportation downtown
U. Liked to read; Dicey's brother
V. Dicey had one from the music teacher requesting a conference
W. Dicey and Wilhemina worked together on a ____ project
X. Dicey bought Sammy a toy ____
Y. Dicey's pot of gold

Dicey's Song Matching 4 Answer Key

S - 1. HONKY
M - 2. GUITAR
J - 3. SAMMY
L - 4. MILLIE
X - 5. ROCKET
O - 6. CRISFIELD
U - 7. JAMES
A - 8. MUSIC
G - 9. ADOPTION
T - 10. BOAT
D - 11. ANGEL
E - 12. READ
Q - 13. VOIGT
R - 14. LINGERLE
P - 15. GRAM
V - 16. NOTE
Y - 17. SAILBOAT
K - 18. JEFF
N - 19. SPOON
H - 20. OCEAN
B - 21. FAT
W - 22. SCIENCE
C - 23. MINA
I - 24. WELFARE
F - 25. APRON

A. Maybeth's talent
B. Mr. Lingerle's physical condition
C. Dicey's school friend
D. Dicey says Maybeth looks like a Christmas ____
E. Dicey wanted James to find a way to help Maybeth ____
F. Everyone laughed at Dicey's ____; her home-ec creation
G. Process by which Gram became guardian of the children
H. Dicey's conversations with Mina were 'like running along the ____'
I. Gram gets these checks
J. Wanted to help Dicey with the boat
K. Played guitar after school
L. Store owner
M. Jeff's instrument
N. Gram sells it to get money to go to Boston
O. Town where Dicey lives
P. Adopted the children
Q. Author
R. Music teacher
S. Mina's friends called Dicey this name
T. Gram's transportation downtown
U. Liked to read; Dicey's brother
V. Dicey had one from the music teacher requesting a conference
W. Dicey and Wilhemina worked together on a ____ project
X. Dicey bought Sammy a toy ____
Y. Dicey's pot of gold

Dicey's Song Magic Squares 1

Match the definition with the vocabulary word. Put your answers in the magic squares below. When your answers are correct, all columns and rows will add to the same number.

A. MINA
B. EVERSLEIGH
C. APRON
D. MUSIC
E. BOX
F. VOIGT
G. MAYBETH
H. MONEY
I. DICEY
J. JOHN
K. HONKY
L. FAT
M. ROCKET
N. BOOTLEGGING
O. CRISFIELD
P. ESSAY

1. Mr. Lingerle gave Gram an envelope with ____ in it
2. Dicey bought Sammy a toy ____
3. Home Ec teacher
4. Mina's friends called Dicey this name
5. Gram's husband
6. Everyone laughed at Dicey's ____; her home-ec creation
7. Mr. Chappelle accused Dicey of plagiarizing her ____
8. The man at the wood store gave Dicey a ____
9. Town where Dicey lives
10. Author
11. Brings the Tillerman children to Crisfield
12. Maybeth's talent
13. Dicey's school friend
14. Mr. Lingerle's physical condition
15. Slow learner; talented musician
16. Former illegal profession of the Tillermans

A=	B=	C=	D=
E=	F=	G=	H=
I=	J=	K=	L=
M=	N=	O=	P=

Dicey's Song Magic Squares 1 Answer Key

Match the definition with the vocabulary word. Put your answers in the magic squares below. When your answers are correct, all columns and rows will add to the same number.

A. MINA
B. EVERSLEIGH
C. APRON
D. MUSIC
E. BOX
F. VOIGT
G. MAYBETH
H. MONEY
I. DICEY
J. JOHN
K. HONKY
L. FAT
M. ROCKET
N. BOOTLEGGING
O. CRISFIELD
P. ESSAY

1. Mr. Lingerle gave Gram an envelope with ____ in it
2. Dicey bought Sammy a toy ____
3. Home Ec teacher
4. Mina's friends called Dicey this name
5. Gram's husband
6. Everyone laughed at Dicey's ____; her home-ec creation
7. Mr. Chappelle accused Dicey of plagiarizing her ____
8. The man at the wood store gave Dicey a ____
9. Town where Dicey lives
10. Author
11. Brings the Tillerman children to Crisfield
12. Maybeth's talent
13. Dicey's school friend
14. Mr. Lingerle's physical condition
15. Slow learner; talented musician
16. Former illegal profession of the Tillermans

A=13	B=3	C=6	D=12
E=8	F=10	G=15	H=1
I=11	J=5	K=4	L=14
M=2	N=16	O=9	P=7

Copyrighted

Dicey's Song Magic Squares 2

Match the definition with the vocabulary word. Put your answers in the magic squares below. When your answers are correct, all columns and rows will add to the same number.

A. LIZA
B. THIRTEEN
C. JEFF
D. READ
E. SAMMY
F. MARBLES
G. HONKY
H. MULBERRY
I. SPOON
J. EVERSLEIGH
K. BOSTON
L. TEN
M. CHAPPELLE
N. WELFARE
O. NOTE
P. ANGEL

1. Dicey's age at the beginning of the book
2. Mina's friends called Dicey this name
3. City where Momma was staying
4. Gram gets these checks
5. English teacher
6. James's age
7. They buried Momma under the paper ____ tree
8. Momma
9. Dicey says Maybeth looks like a Christmas ____
10. Gram sells it to get money to go to Boston
11. Wanted to help Dicey with the boat
12. Dicey wanted James to find a way to help Maybeth ____
13. Played guitar after school
14. Gram won these from the second graders
15. Home Ec teacher
16. Dicey had one from the music teacher requesting a conference

A=	B=	C=	D=
E=	F=	G=	H=
I=	J=	K=	L=
M=	N=	O=	P=

Dicey's Song Magic Squares 2 Answer Key

Match the definition with the vocabulary word. Put your answers in the magic squares below. When your answers are correct, all columns and rows will add to the same number.

A. LIZA
B. THIRTEEN
C. JEFF
D. READ
E. SAMMY
F. MARBLES
G. HONKY
H. MULBERRY
I. SPOON
J. EVERSLEIGH
K. BOSTON
L. TEN
M. CHAPPELLE
N. WELFARE
O. NOTE
P. ANGEL

1. Dicey's age at the beginning of the book
2. Mina's friends called Dicey this name
3. City where Momma was staying
4. Gram gets these checks
5. English teacher
6. James's age
7. They buried Momma under the paper ____ tree
8. Momma
9. Dicey says Maybeth looks like a Christmas ____
10. Gram sells it to get money to go to Boston
11. Wanted to help Dicey with the boat
12. Dicey wanted James to find a way to help Maybeth ____
13. Played guitar after school
14. Gram won these from the second graders
15. Home Ec teacher
16. Dicey had one from the music teacher requesting a conference

A=8	B=1	C=13	D=12
E=11	F=14	G=2	H=7
I=10	J=15	K=3	L=6
M=5	N=4	O=16	P=9

Dicey's Song Magic Squares 3

Match the definition with the vocabulary word. Put your answers in the magic squares below. When your answers are correct, all columns and rows will add to the same number.

A. MONEY
B. SEVEN
C. MUSIC
D. ADOPTION
E. VOIGT
F. MILLIE
G. ATTIC
H. LIZA
I. BOX
J. LINGERLE
K. SCIENCE
L. SAILBOAT
M. MINA
N. HONKY
O. OCEAN
P. GUITAR

1. Momma
2. Mr. Lingerle gave Gram an envelope with ____ in it
3. Sammy's age
4. The children got into trouble looking at things in Gram's ____
5. Music teacher
6. Dicey's conversations with Mina were 'like running along the ____'
7. Jeff's instrument
8. The man at the wood store gave Dicey a ____
9. Dicey and Wilhemina worked together on a ____ project
10. Mina's friends called Dicey this name
11. Dicey's school friend
12. Dicey's pot of gold
13. Author
14. Process by which Gram became guardian of the children
15. Maybeth's talent
16. Store owner

A=	B=	C=	D=
E=	F=	G=	H=
I=	J=	K=	L=
M=	N=	O=	P=

Dicey's Song Magic Squares 3 Answer Key

Match the definition with the vocabulary word. Put your answers in the magic squares below. When your answers are correct, all columns and rows will add to the same number.

A. MONEY
B. SEVEN
C. MUSIC
D. ADOPTION
E. VOIGT
F. MILLIE
G. ATTIC
H. LIZA
I. BOX
J. LINGERLE
K. SCIENCE
L. SAILBOAT
M. MINA
N. HONKY
O. OCEAN
P. GUITAR

1. Momma
2. Mr. Lingerle gave Gram an envelope with ____ in it
3. Sammy's age
4. The children got into trouble looking at things in Gram's ____
5. Music teacher
6. Dicey's conversations with Mina were 'like running along the ____'
7. Jeff's instrument
8. The man at the wood store gave Dicey a ____
9. Dicey and Wilhemina worked together on a ____ project
10. Mina's friends called Dicey this name
11. Dicey's school friend
12. Dicey's pot of gold
13. Author
14. Process by which Gram became guardian of the children
15. Maybeth's talent
16. Store owner

A=2	B=3	C=15	D=14
E=13	F=16	G=4	H=1
I=8	J=5	K=9	L=12
M=11	N=10	O=6	P=7

Dicey's Song Magic Squares 4

Match the definition with the vocabulary word. Put your answers in the magic squares below. When your answers are correct, all columns and rows will add to the same number.

A. BOOTLEGGING
B. CHAPPELLE
C. MAYBETH
D. CRISFIELD
E. ANGEL
F. HONKY
G. MUSIC
H. MINA
I. ATTIC
J. NOTE
K. BOSTON
L. SAMMY
M. DICEY
N. FAT
O. BOAT
P. MONEY

1. Gram's transportation downtown
2. Dicey had one from the music teacher requesting a conference
3. Dicey's school friend
4. Former illegal profession of the Tillermans
5. Town where Dicey lives
6. Dicey says Maybeth looks like a Christmas ____
7. City where Momma was staying
8. Mr. Lingerle's physical condition
9. Mina's friends called Dicey this name
10. Slow learner; talented musician
11. Brings the Tillerman children to Crisfield
12. Wanted to help Dicey with the boat
13. The children got into trouble looking at things in Gram's ____
14. Mr. Lingerle gave Gram an envelope with ____ in it
15. English teacher
16. Maybeth's talent

A=	B=	C=	D=
E=	F=	G=	H=
I=	J=	K=	L=
M=	N=	O=	P=

27
Copyrighted

Dicey's Song Magic Squares 4 Answer Key

Match the definition with the vocabulary word. Put your answers in the magic squares below. When your answers are correct, all columns and rows will add to the same number.

A. BOOTLEGGING
B. CHAPPELLE
C. MAYBETH
D. CRISFIELD
E. ANGEL
F. HONKY
G. MUSIC
H. MINA
I. ATTIC
J. NOTE
K. BOSTON
L. SAMMY
M. DICEY
N. FAT
O. BOAT
P. MONEY

1. Gram's transportation downtown
2. Dicey had one from the music teacher requesting a conference
3. Dicey's school friend
4. Former illegal profession of the Tillermans
5. Town where Dicey lives
6. Dicey says Maybeth looks like a Christmas ____
7. City where Momma was staying
8. Mr. Lingerle's physical condition
9. Mina's friends called Dicey this name
10. Slow learner; talented musician
11. Brings the Tillerman children to Crisfield
12. Wanted to help Dicey with the boat
13. The children got into trouble looking at things in Gram's ____
14. Mr. Lingerle gave Gram an envelope with ____ in it
15. English teacher
16. Maybeth's talent

A=4	B=15	C=10	D=5
E=6	F=9	G=16	H=3
I=13	J=2	K=7	L=12
M=11	N=8	O=1	P=14

28
Copyrighted

Dicey's Song Word Search 1

Words are placed backwards, forward, diagonally, up and down. Clues listed below can help you find the words. Circle the hidden vocabulary words in the maze.

```
M J O H N G H K Q S D Q X C S D R Q
A P X S T O D O E Q C Q R A I A T Q
R O M T A G T V N W V I M C T S H D
B O S T O N E E Q K S M E I F N I R
L H B C B N R S J F Y Y U N O Z R N
E K E C D X A L I B K G G I C W T H
S A Y Y N R F E L I Z A T N N E E S
N D Y O W S L W H C K P V O L D E N
F D O L S D E W C Z O L R G C P N Y
M P F M W X W Z H D D P X R J B A B
S A I L B O A T A Z A C M O Y S G J
W A L M B H H C P Q R C U C S Q W L
D W N B I V Q X P P T Z L E N J N F
G P D G O L N Q E J D M B R M A W G
D F C I E S L C L V O W E Y I M D C
P A G W N L B I L N T P R G N E I X
A T T I C N E T E K C O R J A S C Z
J E F F W N R Y R J Q A Y W U X K C
M A Y B E T H J J W M S G M R E A D
```

Adopted the children (4)
Author (5)
Brings the Tillerman children to Crisfield (5)
City where Momma was staying (6)
Dicey and Wilhemina worked together on a _____ project (7)
Dicey bought Sammy a toy _____ (6)
Dicey had one from the music teacher requesting a conference (4)
Dicey says Maybeth looks like a Christmas _____ (5)
Dicey wanted James to find a way to help Maybeth _____ (4)
Dicey's age at the beginning of the book (8)
Dicey's conversations with Mina were 'like running along the _____' (5)
Dicey's pot of gold (8)
Dicey's school friend (4)
English teacher (9)
Everyone laughed at Dicey's _____; her home-ec creation (5)
Gram gets these checks (7)
Gram sells it to get money to go to Boston (5)
Gram won these from the second graders (7)
Gram's husband (4)
Gram's transportation downtown (4)

James's age (3)
Jeff's instrument (6)
Liked to read; Dicey's brother (5)
Maybeth's talent (5)
Millie owned a _____ store (7)
Mina's friends called Dicey this name (5)
Momma (4)
Mr. Chappelle accused Dicey of plagiarizing her _____ (5)
Mr. Lingerle gave Gram an envelope with _____ in it (5)
Mr. Lingerle's physical condition (3)
Played guitar after school (4)
Process by which Gram became guardian of the children (8)
Sammy's age (5)
Slow learner; talented musician (7)
Store owner (6)
The children got into trouble looking at things in Gram's _____ (5)
The man at the wood store gave Dicey a _____ (3)
They buried Momma under the paper _____ tree (8)
Town where Dicey lives (9)
Wanted to help Dicey with the boat (5)

Dicey's Song Word Search 1 Answer Key

Words are placed backwards, forward, diagonally, up and down. Clues listed below can help you find the words. Circle the hidden vocabulary words in the maze.

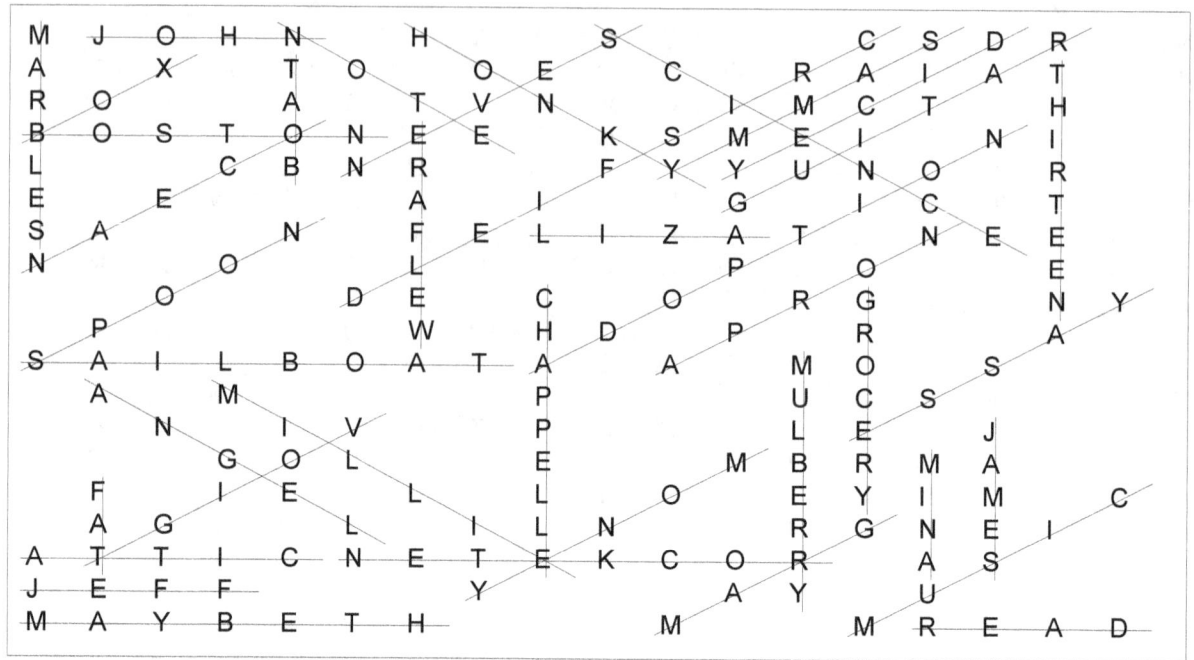

Adopted the children (4)
Author (5)
Brings the Tillerman children to Crisfield (5)
City where Momma was staying (6)
Dicey and Wilhemina worked together on a ____ project (7)
Dicey bought Sammy a toy ____ (6)
Dicey had one from the music teacher requesting a conference (4)
Dicey says Maybeth looks like a Christmas ____ (5)
Dicey wanted James to find a way to help Maybeth ____ (4)
Dicey's age at the beginning of the book (8)
Dicey's conversations with Mina were 'like running along the ____' (5)
Dicey's pot of gold (8)
Dicey's school friend (4)
English teacher (9)
Everyone laughed at Dicey's ____; her home-ec creation (5)
Gram gets these checks (7)
Gram sells it to get money to go to Boston (5)
Gram won these from the second graders (7)
Gram's husband (4)
Gram's transportation downtown (4)

James's age (3)
Jeff's instrument (6)
Liked to read; Dicey's brother (5)
Maybeth's talent (5)
Millie owned a ____ store (7)
Mina's friends called Dicey this name (5)
Momma (4)
Mr. Chappelle accused Dicey of plagiarizing her ____ (5)
Mr. Lingerle gave Gram an envelope with ____ in it (5)
Mr. Lingerle's physical condition (3)
Played guitar after school (4)
Process by which Gram became guardian of the children (8)
Sammy's age (5)
Slow learner; talented musician (7)
Store owner (6)
The children got into trouble looking at things in Gram's ____ (5)
The man at the wood store gave Dicey a ____ (3)
They buried Momma under the paper ____ tree (8)
Town where Dicey lives (9)
Wanted to help Dicey with the boat (5)

Dicey's Song Word Search 2

Words are placed backwards, forward, diagonally, up and down. Clues listed below can help you find the words. Circle the hidden vocabulary words in the maze.

```
E S L S G M U L B E R R Y G T S M J
S P C Q A U J D X G F M M D H C A V
S O B H T I I R J X M U I B I I R F
A O F G A P L T O P Z S L O R E B L
Y N I Q M P M B A C Y I L S T N L V
Y O B B V L P T O R K C I T E C E Z
V W Y G F W I E W A M E E O E E S Q
V E K P S W J N L P T M T N N K F Y
P L L W H V V G G L K C A R F R W X
Q F X G P M Q Z G E E K D Y X G C W
T A D D M J G K R Y R G I T B G I W
J R A G O M H T A P Y L C S T E T P
S E V E N Y Y Z M G M M E G E T T S
R A F B E O P T H C M M Y R N A A H
V P M F Y K T T O D A F M O F O P M
Q R Z G Q H N E N J S V I C G B K T
N O I T P O D A K D G W N E J O H N
L N B C M Z G T Y L P Q A R Q D G S
O C E A N L I Z A N G E L Y T V K D
```

Adopted the children (4)
Author (5)
Brings the Tillerman children to Crisfield (5)
City where Momma was staying (6)
Dicey and Wilhemina worked together on a ____ project (7)
Dicey bought Sammy a toy ____ (6)
Dicey had one from the music teacher requesting a conference (4)
Dicey says Maybeth looks like a Christmas ____ (5)
Dicey wanted James to find a way to help Maybeth ____ (4)
Dicey's age at the beginning of the book (8)
Dicey's conversations with Mina were 'like running along the ____' (5)
Dicey's pot of gold (8)
Dicey's school friend (4)
English teacher (9)
Everyone laughed at Dicey's ____; her home-ec creation (5)
Gram gets these checks (7)
Gram sells it to get money to go to Boston (5)
Gram won these from the second graders (7)
Gram's husband (4)
Gram's transportation downtown (4)

James's age (3)
Jeff's instrument (6)
Liked to read; Dicey's brother (5)
Maybeth's talent (5)
Millie owned a ____ store (7)
Mina's friends called Dicey this name (5)
Momma (4)
Mr. Chappelle accused Dicey of plagiarizing her ____ (5)
Mr. Lingerle gave Gram an envelope with ____ in it (5)
Mr. Lingerle's physical condition (3)
Music teacher (8)
Played guitar after school (4)
Process by which Gram became guardian of the children (8)
Sammy's age (5)
Slow learner; talented musician (7)
Store owner (6)
The children got into trouble looking at things in Gram's ____ (5)
The man at the wood store gave Dicey a ____ (3)
They buried Momma under the paper ____ tree (8)
Wanted to help Dicey with the boat (5)

Dicey's Song Word Search 2 Answer Key

Words are placed backwards, forward, diagonally, up and down. Clues listed below can help you find the words. Circle the hidden vocabulary words in the maze.

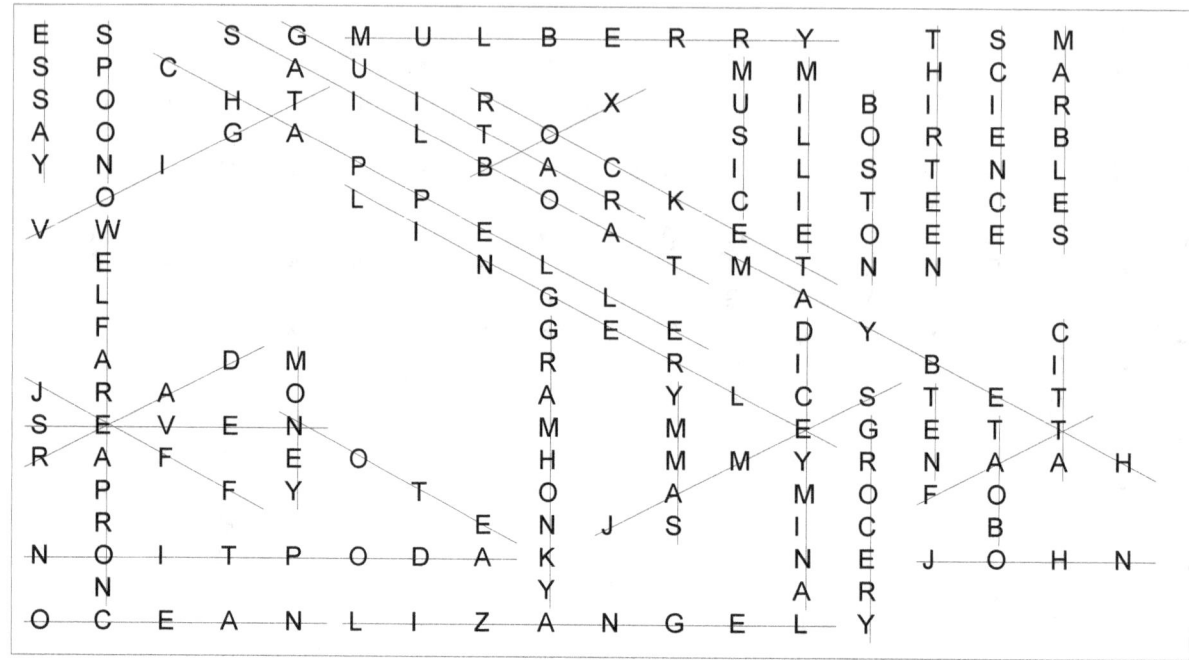

Adopted the children (4)
Author (5)
Brings the Tillerman children to Crisfield (5)
City where Momma was staying (6)
Dicey and Wilhemina worked together on a ____ project (7)
Dicey bought Sammy a toy ____ (6)
Dicey had one from the music teacher requesting a conference (4)
Dicey says Maybeth looks like a Christmas ____ (5)
Dicey wanted James to find a way to help Maybeth ____ (4)
Dicey's age at the beginning of the book (8)
Dicey's conversations with Mina were 'like running along the ____' (5)
Dicey's pot of gold (8)
Dicey's school friend (4)
English teacher (9)
Everyone laughed at Dicey's ____; her home-ec creation (5)
Gram gets these checks (7)
Gram sells it to get money to go to Boston (5)
Gram won these from the second graders (7)
Gram's husband (4)
Gram's transportation downtown (4)

James's age (3)
Jeff's instrument (6)
Liked to read; Dicey's brother (5)
Maybeth's talent (5)
Millie owned a ____ store (7)
Mina's friends called Dicey this name (5)
Momma (4)
Mr. Chappelle accused Dicey of plagiarizing her ____ (5)
Mr. Lingerle gave Gram an envelope with ____ in it (5)
Mr. Lingerle's physical condition (3)
Music teacher (8)
Played guitar after school (4)
Process by which Gram became guardian of the children (8)
Sammy's age (5)
Slow learner; talented musician (7)
Store owner (6)
The children got into trouble looking at things in Gram's ____ (5)
The man at the wood store gave Dicey a ____ (3)
They buried Momma under the paper ____ tree (8)
Wanted to help Dicey with the boat (5)

Dicey's Song Word Search 3

Words are placed backwards, forward, diagonally, up and down. Words listed below are included in the maze. Circle the hidden vocabulary words in the maze.

```
N O T S O B X S A D O P T I O N T V
X O Y L W W N C T G L C S N W Y M H
S K T B I W P I H U F B P J X S X M
S H Y E X Z N E I I G R O C E R Y Q
D S Z C Z D A N R T Z O O M N A L G
N A H S I T L C T A W C N U N N Z Z
C M W C T L K E E R T K C S J G H E
P M E I M Y X B E E P E D I O E I S
L Y C W M Y H O N K Y T M C D L H X
H M F H A B Z O V X G A E B L T M S
H Q I S A X R F L I R A F I E B U X
J K S N D P R T O B N F M B I L L N
N E J K A S P V L J E Y Y W F I B J
P B O Q E E X E X J E A M E S N E N
B M H J R V S Z L N M J B L I G R P
T O N T D E R B O L F A T F R E R Q
P D A W C N Z M O M E M X A C R Y M
H F S T V L W T J X V E M R V L G T
E V E R S L E I G H Y S C E J E V F
```

ADOPTION	EVERSLEIGH	MARBLES	SAMMY
ANGEL	FAT	MAYBETH	SCIENCE
APRON	GRAM	MILLIE	SEVEN
ATTIC	GROCERY	MINA	SPOON
BOAT	GUITAR	MONEY	TEN
BOSTON	HONKY	MULBERRY	THIRTEEN
BOX	JAMES	MUSIC	VOIGT
CHAPPELLE	JEFF	NOTE	WELFARE
CRISFIELD	JOHN	OCEAN	
DICEY	LINGERLE	READ	
ESSAY	LIZA	ROCKET	

Dicey's Song Word Search 3 Answer Key

Words are placed backwards, forward, diagonally, up and down. Words listed below are included in the maze. Circle the hidden vocabulary words in the maze.

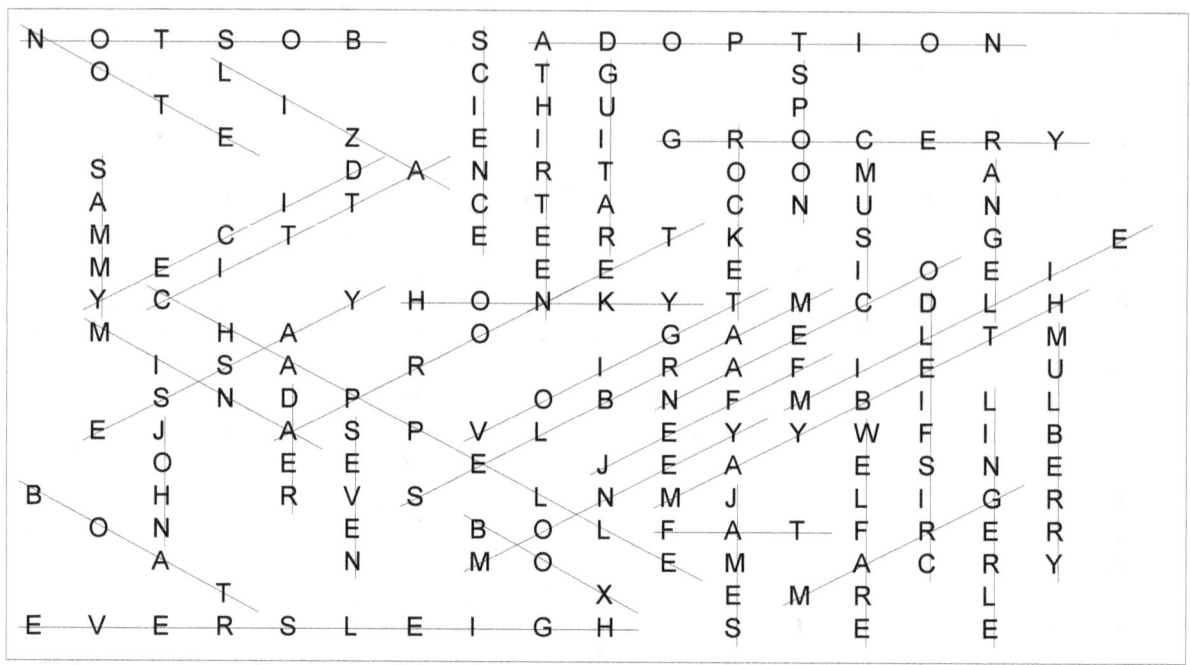

ADOPTION	EVERSLEIGH	MARBLES	SAMMY
ANGEL	FAT	MAYBETH	SCIENCE
APRON	GRAM	MILLIE	SEVEN
ATTIC	GROCERY	MINA	SPOON
BOAT	GUITAR	MONEY	TEN
BOSTON	HONKY	MULBERRY	THIRTEEN
BOX	JAMES	MUSIC	VOIGT
CHAPPELLE	JEFF	NOTE	WELFARE
CRISFIELD	JOHN	OCEAN	
DICEY	LINGERLE	READ	
ESSAY	LIZA	ROCKET	

Dicey's Song Word Search 4

Words are placed backwards, forward, diagonally, up and down. Words listed below are included in the maze. Circle the hidden vocabulary words in the maze.

```
B H M J O A C B K C R I S F I E L D
O B A R C N V O L Y D O B W T V S S
O J R P E G R S V W J S C D G P A C
T B B V A E T T J H B R K K C Z I K
L M L G N L H O N K Y P Y H E M L T
E G E I R X K N P S L R D W I T B Z
G L S R N A B E Z M E M P L B M O J
G V Y A P G M E L C W N L P I N A R
I M O T C V E T O W Y I J N S E T H
N H G I E L S R E V E R A F L E W Q
G L S U G Y G I L N N K E L P C Y R
G U H G D T C H X E O P E A A J V J
M J J T I J Y T S R M P W E D B N K
H A E X C O P A X A P F C J O A O T
K M F L E H V O Y A M N A C P P S X
H E F G Y N Z B H L E M I T T R E D
M S P O O N E C N I I T Y L I O V Y
S F T T J T F L C L T Z B S O N E W
N H E B H B E S S A Y Y A L N X N N
```

ADOPTION	ESSAY	LIZA	SAILBOAT
ANGEL	EVERSLEIGH	MARBLES	SAMMY
APRON	FAT	MAYBETH	SCIENCE
ATTIC	GRAM	MILLIE	SEVEN
BOAT	GROCERY	MINA	SPOON
BOOTLEGGING	GUITAR	MONEY	TEN
BOSTON	HONKY	MUSIC	THIRTEEN
BOX	JAMES	NOTE	VOIGT
CHAPPELLE	JEFF	OCEAN	WELFARE
CRISFIELD	JOHN	READ	
DICEY	LINGERLE	ROCKET	

Dicey's Song Word Search 4 Answer Key

Words are placed backwards, forward, diagonally, up and down. Words listed below are included in the maze. Circle the hidden vocabulary words in the maze.

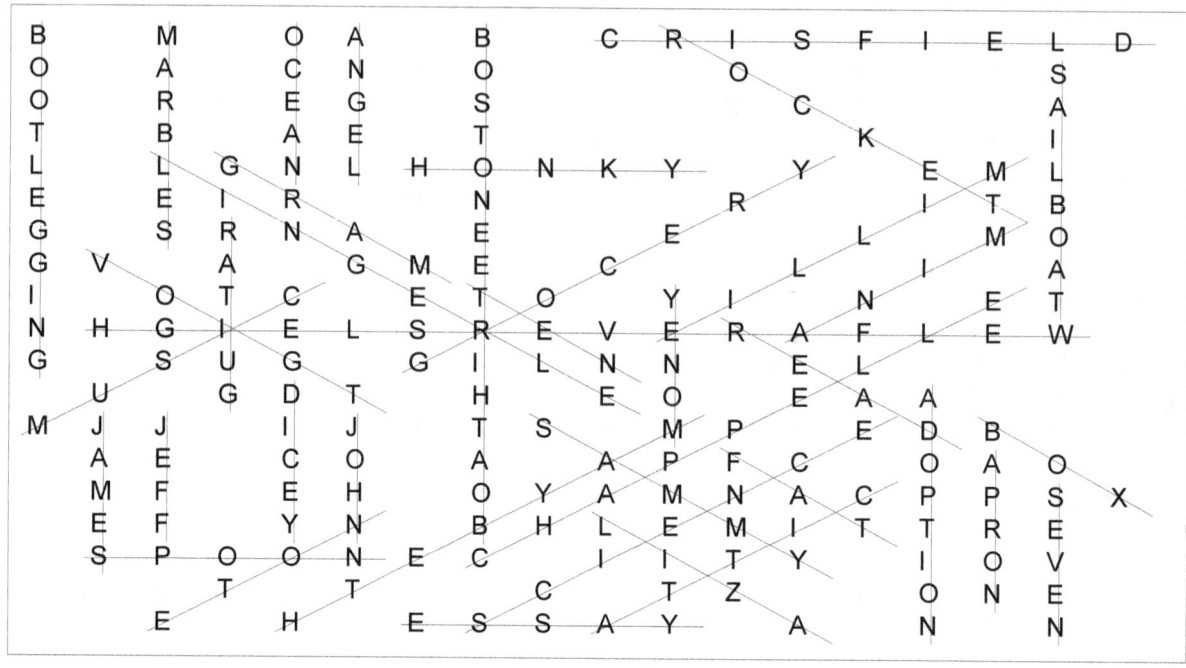

ADOPTION	ESSAY	LIZA	SAILBOAT
ANGEL	EVERSLEIGH	MARBLES	SAMMY
APRON	FAT	MAYBETH	SCIENCE
ATTIC	GRAM	MILLIE	SEVEN
BOAT	GROCERY	MINA	SPOON
BOOTLEGGING	GUITAR	MONEY	TEN
BOSTON	HONKY	MUSIC	THIRTEEN
BOX	JAMES	NOTE	VOIGT
CHAPPELLE	JEFF	OCEAN	WELFARE
CRISFIELD	JOHN	READ	
DICEY	LINGERLE	ROCKET	

Dicey's Song Crossword 1

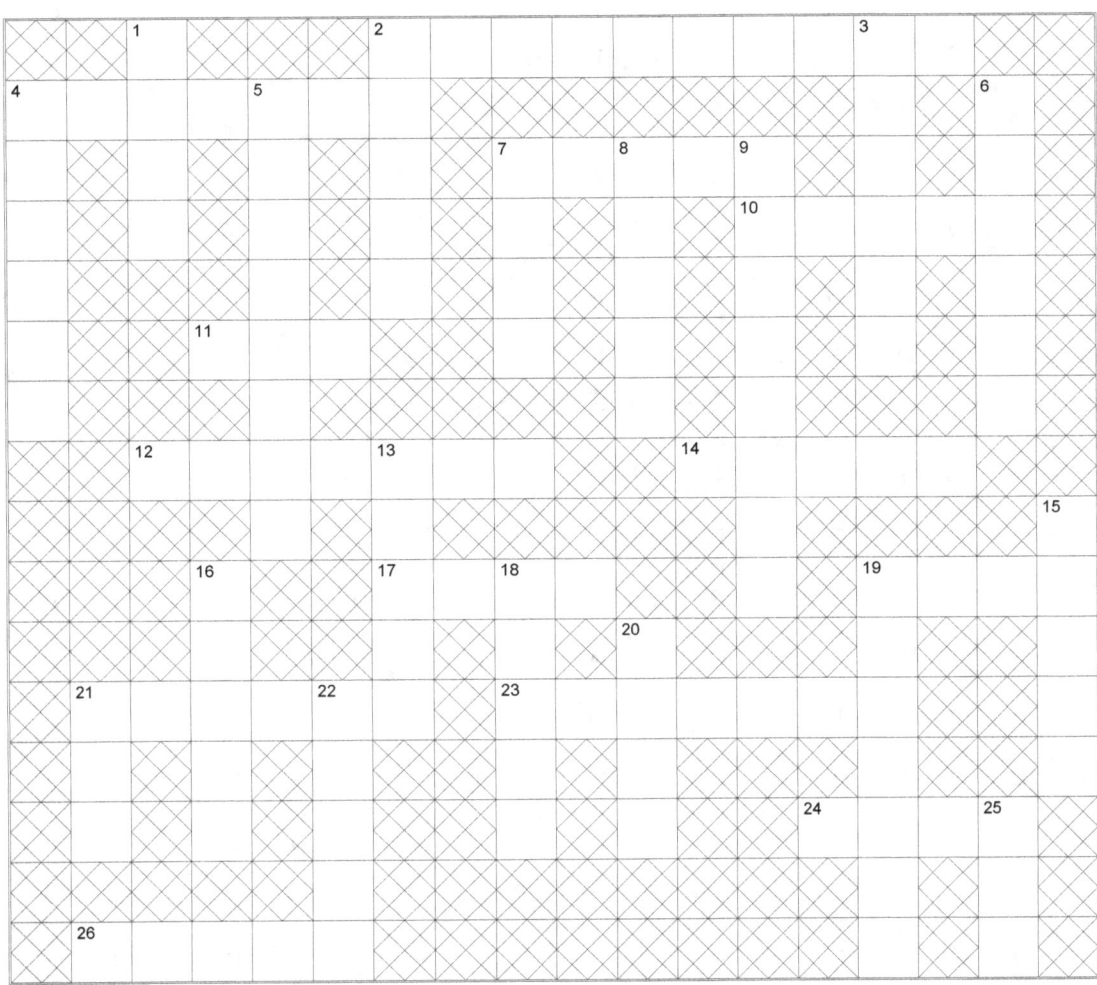

Across
2. Home Ec teacher
4. Gram won these from the second graders
7. Liked to read; Dicey's brother
10. The children got into trouble looking at things in Gram's ____
11. James's age
12. Gram gets these checks
14. Mina's friends called Dicey this name
17. Dicey wanted James to find a way to help Maybeth ____
19. Dicey's school friend
21. City where Momma was staying
23. Millie owned a ____ store
24. Played guitar after school
26. Sammy's age

Down
1. Adopted the children
2. Mr. Chappelle accused Dicey of plagiarizing her ____
3. Jeff's instrument
4. Store owner
5. Music teacher
6. Dicey bought Sammy a toy ____
7. Gram's husband
8. Mr. Lingerle gave Gram an envelope with ____ in it
9. Dicey's pot of gold
13. Everyone laughed at Dicey's ____; her home-ec creation
15. Wanted to help Dicey with the boat
16. Maybeth's talent
18. Dicey says Maybeth looks like a Christmas ____
19. Slow learner; talented musician
20. Dicey had one from the music teacher requesting a conference
21. The man at the wood store gave Dicey a ____
22. Dicey's conversations with Mina were 'like running along the ____'
25. Mr. Lingerle's physical condition

Dicey's Song Crossword 1 Answer Key

	1		2						3	
	G		E	V	E	R	S	L	E	I	G	H
4		5								6
M	A	R	B	L	E	S			U	R
I		A			7	8		9		O
					J	A	M	E	S	
L		M			O		O	10		
								A	T	T	I	C
L					H		N	I		K
	11									
I	T	E	N		N		E	L		R	E
E		R					Y	B		T
	12			13			14			
	W	E	L	F	A	R	E	H	O	N	K	Y
				E				A		15
	16		17		18		19			S
	M		R	E	A	D	T		M	I	N	A
	U				N		A			M
21		22			23					
B	O	S	T	O	N	G	R	O	C	E	R	Y
O		I			E		T			B		M
X		C			L		E		24	J	25 F
											A
26										T
S	E	V	E	N					H		T

Across
2. Home Ec teacher
4. Gram won these from the second graders
7. Liked to read; Dicey's brother
10. The children got into trouble looking at things in Gram's ____
11. James's age
12. Gram gets these checks
14. Mina's friends called Dicey this name
17. Dicey wanted James to find a way to help Maybeth ____
19. Dicey's school friend
21. City where Momma was staying
23. Millie owned a ____ store
24. Played guitar after school
26. Sammy's age

Down
1. Adopted the children
2. Mr. Chappelle accused Dicey of plagiarizing her ____
3. Jeff's instrument
4. Store owner
5. Music teacher
6. Dicey bought Sammy a toy ____
7. Gram's husband
8. Mr. Lingerle gave Gram an envelope with ____ in it
9. Dicey's pot of gold
13. Everyone laughed at Dicey's ____; her home-ec creation
15. Wanted to help Dicey with the boat
16. Maybeth's talent
18. Dicey says Maybeth looks like a Christmas ____
19. Slow learner; talented musician
20. Dicey had one from the music teacher requesting a conference
21. The man at the wood store gave Dicey a ____
22. Dicey's conversations with Mina were 'like running along the ____'
25. Mr. Lingerle's physical condition

Dicey's Song Crossword 2

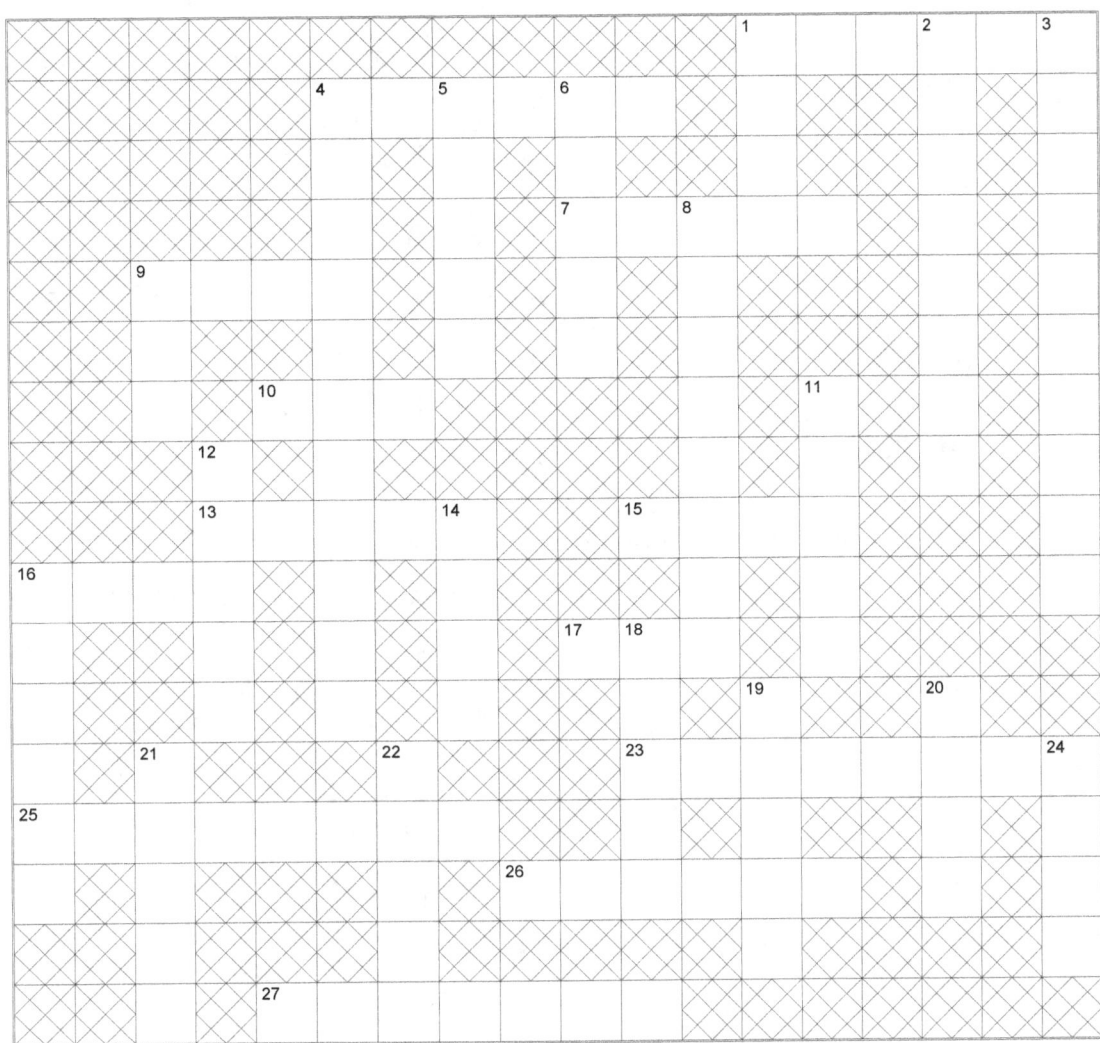

Across
1. Store owner
4. City where Momma was staying
7. Mr. Chappelle accused Dicey of plagiarizing her ____
9. Gram's transportation downtown
10. James's age
13. Dicey says Maybeth looks like a Christmas ____
15. Gram's husband
16. Adopted the children
17. Mr. Lingerle's physical condition
23. Dicey's age at the beginning of the book
25. Process by which Gram became guardian of the children
26. Dicey bought Sammy a toy ____
27. Slow learner; talented musician

Down
1. Dicey's school friend
2. Music teacher
3. Home Ec teacher
4. Former illegal profession of the Tillermans
5. Gram sells it to get money to go to Boston
6. Dicey's conversations with Mina were 'like running along the ____'
8. Dicey's pot of gold
9. The man at the wood store gave Dicey a ____
11. Mr. Lingerle gave Gram an envelope with ____ in it
12. Liked to read; Dicey's brother
14. Momma
16. Jeff's instrument
18. The children got into trouble looking at things in Gram's ____
19. Brings the Tillerman children to Crisfield
20. Played guitar after school
21. Author
22. Mina's friends called Dicey this name
24. Dicey had one from the music teacher requesting a conference

Dicey's Song Crossword 2 Answer Key

									1 M	I	2 L	L	3 E
			4 B	O	5 S	T	6 O	N	I		I		V
			O		P		C		N		N		E
			O		O		7 E	S	8 S	A	Y		G	E	R
		9 B	O	A	T		O		A		A			E		S
		O			L		N		N		I			R		L
		X		10 T	E	N				L		11 M		L		E
			12 J		G					B		O		E		I
			13 A	N	G	E	14 L		15 J	O	H	N				G
16 G	R	A	M		I		I			A		E				H
U			E		N		Z		17 F	18 A	T	Y				
I			S		G		A			T			19 D		20 J	
T		21 V			22 H				23 T	H	I	R	T	E	E	24 N
25 A	D	O	P	T	I	O	N			I			C		F		O
R		I			N		26 R	O	C	K	E	T		F		T
		G			K					Y						E
		T		27 M	A	Y	B	E	T	H						

Across
1. Store owner
4. City where Momma was staying
7. Mr. Chappelle accused Dicey of plagiarizing her ____
9. Gram's transportation downtown
10. James's age
13. Dicey says Maybeth looks like a Christmas ____
15. Gram's husband
16. Adopted the children
17. Mr. Lingerle's physical condition
23. Dicey's age at the beginning of the book
25. Process by which Gram became guardian of the children
26. Dicey bought Sammy a toy ____
27. Slow learner; talented musician

Down
1. Dicey's school friend
2. Music teacher
3. Home Ec teacher
4. Former illegal profession of the Tillermans
5. Gram sells it to get money to go to Boston
6. Dicey's conversations with Mina were 'like running along the ____'
8. Dicey's pot of gold
9. The man at the wood store gave Dicey a ____
11. Mr. Lingerle gave Gram an envelope with ____ in it
12. Liked to read; Dicey's brother
14. Momma
16. Jeff's instrument
18. The children got into trouble looking at things in Gram's ____
19. Brings the Tillerman children to Crisfield
20. Played guitar after school
21. Author
22. Mina's friends called Dicey this name
24. Dicey had one from the music teacher requesting a conference

Dicey's Song Crossword 3

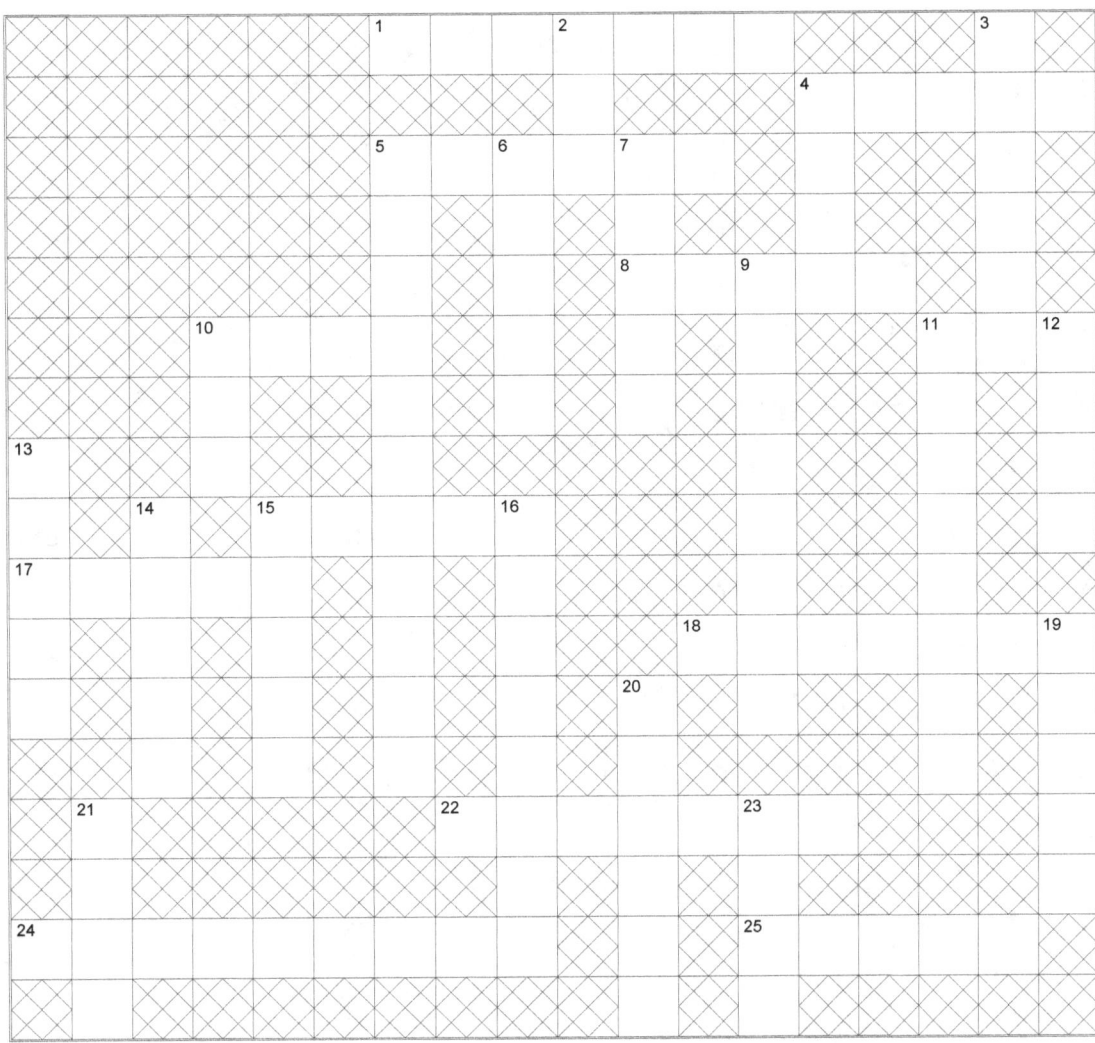

Across
1. Gram gets these checks
4. Maybeth's talent
5. City where Momma was staying
8. Mr. Chappelle accused Dicey of plagiarizing her ____
10. Gram's transportation downtown
11. James's age
15. Dicey says Maybeth looks like a Christmas ____
17. Author
18. Slow learner; talented musician
22. Millie owned a ____ store
24. English teacher
25. Everyone laughed at Dicey's ____; her home-ec creation

Down
2. Mr. Lingerle's physical condition
3. Store owner
4. Dicey's school friend
5. Former illegal profession of the Tillermans
6. Gram sells it to get money to go to Boston
7. Dicey's conversations with Mina were 'like running along the ____'
9. Dicey's pot of gold
10. The man at the wood store gave Dicey a ____
11. Dicey's age at the beginning of the book
12. Dicey had one from the music teacher requesting a conference
13. Sammy's age
14. Brings the Tillerman children to Crisfield
15. The children got into trouble looking at things in Gram's ____
16. Music teacher
19. Mina's friends called Dicey this name
20. Dicey bought Sammy a toy ____
21. Gram's husband
23. Dicey wanted James to find a way to help Maybeth ____

Dicey's Song Crossword 3 Answer Key

					1 W	E	L	2 F	A	R	E			3 M	
								A				4 M	U	S	I C
				5 B	O	6 S	T	7 O	N		I		L	
				O		P		C			N		L	
				O		O		8 E	S	9 S	A	Y	I	
			10 B	O	A	T		O		A		11 T	E	12 N
			O			L		N		I		H		O
13 S		X		E					L		I		T
E	14 D	15 A	N	G	16 E	L			B		R		E
17 V	O	I	G	T		G		I		O		T	
E		C		T		I		N		18 M	A	Y	B	E	T	19 H
N		E		I		N		G		20 R	T		E		O
		Y		C		G		E		O			N		N
	21 J				22 G	R	O	C	E	23 R	Y			K
	O					L		K		E			Y
24 C	H	A	P	P	E	L	L	E		25 A	P	R	O	N
	N							T		D			

Across
1. Gram gets these checks
4. Maybeth's talent
5. City where Momma was staying
8. Mr. Chappelle accused Dicey of plagiarizing her ____
10. Gram's transportation downtown
11. James's age
15. Dicey says Maybeth looks like a Christmas ____
17. Author
18. Slow learner; talented musician
22. Millie owned a ____ store
24. English teacher
25. Everyone laughed at Dicey's ____; her home-ec creation

Down
2. Mr. Lingerle's physical condition
3. Store owner
4. Dicey's school friend
5. Former illegal profession of the Tillermans
6. Gram sells it to get money to go to Boston
7. Dicey's conversations with Mina were 'like running along the ____'
9. Dicey's pot of gold
10. The man at the wood store gave Dicey a ____
11. Dicey's age at the beginning of the book
12. Dicey had one from the music teacher requesting a conference
13. Sammy's age
14. Brings the Tillerman children to Crisfield
15. The children got into trouble looking at things in Gram's ____
16. Music teacher
19. Mina's friends called Dicey this name
20. Dicey bought Sammy a toy ____
21. Gram's husband
23. Dicey wanted James to find a way to help Maybeth ____

Dicey's Song Crossword 4

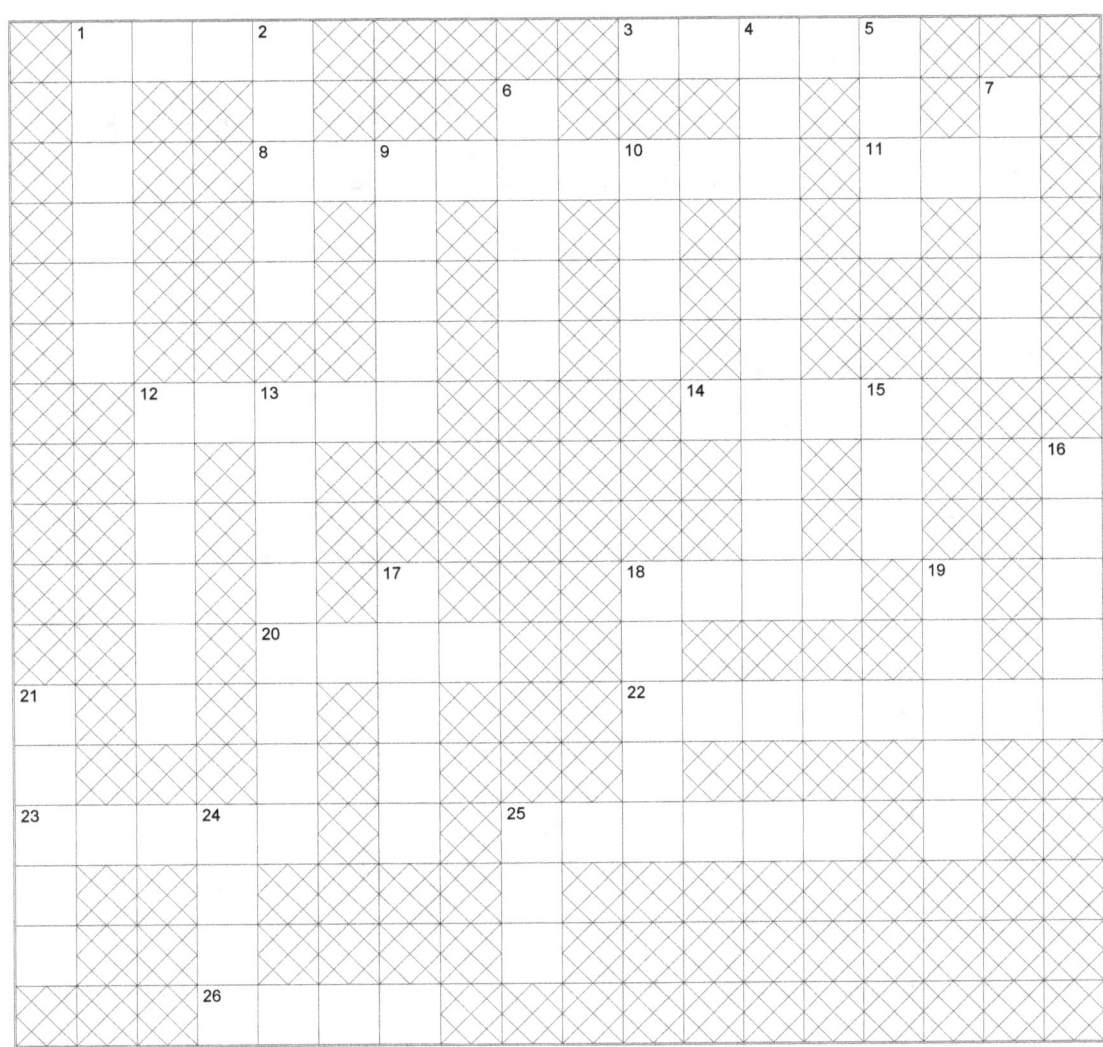

Across
1. Dicey wanted James to find a way to help Maybeth ____
3. Dicey's conversations with Mina were 'like running along the ____'
8. English teacher
11. James's age
12. Maybeth's talent
14. Played guitar after school
18. Gram's husband
20. Gram's transportation downtown
22. They buried Momma under the paper ____ tree
23. Author
25. City where Momma was staying
26. Dicey's school friend

Down
1. Dicey bought Sammy a toy ____
2. Brings the Tillerman children to Crisfield
4. Home Ec teacher
5. Dicey had one from the music teacher requesting a conference
6. Gram sells it to get money to go to Boston
7. Dicey says Maybeth looks like a Christmas ____
9. The children got into trouble looking at things in Gram's ____
10. Momma
12. Store owner
13. Dicey's pot of gold
15. Mr. Lingerle's physical condition
16. Mr. Chappelle accused Dicey of plagiarizing her ____
17. Wanted to help Dicey with the boat
18. Liked to read; Dicey's brother
19. Everyone laughed at Dicey's ____; her home-ec creation
21. Sammy's age
24. Adopted the children
25. The man at the wood store gave Dicey a ____

Dicey's Song Crossword 4 Answer Key

	1 R	E	A	2 D			3 O	4 C	5 E	A	N	
	O			I		6 S		V	O		A	7 A
	C		8 C	H	9 A	P	P	10 E	L	11 L	E	N
	K		E		T		O	L		E		G
	E		Y		T		O	I		T		E
	T				I		N	Z		S		L
		12 M	13 U	S	I	C		A	14 J	E	15 F	F
		I		A					I		A	16 E
		L		I					G		T	S
		L		17 L			18 J	O	H	N	19 A	S
		I		20 B	O	A	T				P	A
21 S		E		O			22 M	U	L	B	E	R	Y
E				A			M				O	
23 V	O	24 I	G	T		25 B	O	S	T	O	N	
E		R				O						
N		A				X						
	26 M	I	N	A								

Across
1. Dicey wanted James to find a way to help Maybeth ____
3. Dicey's conversations with Mina were 'like running along the ____'
8. English teacher
11. James's age
12. Maybeth's talent
14. Played guitar after school
18. Gram's husband
20. Gram's transportation downtown
22. They buried Momma under the paper ____ tree
23. Author
25. City where Momma was staying
26. Dicey's school friend

Down
1. Dicey bought Sammy a toy ____
2. Brings the Tillerman children to Crisfield
4. Home Ec teacher
5. Dicey had one from the music teacher requesting a conference
6. Gram sells it to get money to go to Boston
7. Dicey says Maybeth looks like a Christmas ____
9. The children got into trouble looking at things in Gram's ____
10. Momma
12. Store owner
13. Dicey's pot of gold
15. Mr. Lingerle's physical condition
16. Mr. Chappelle accused Dicey of plagiarizing her ____
17. Wanted to help Dicey with the boat
18. Liked to read; Dicey's brother
19. Everyone laughed at Dicey's ____; her home-ec creation
21. Sammy's age
24. Adopted the children
25. The man at the wood store gave Dicey a ____

Dicey's Song

EVERSLEIGH	SAILBOAT	SCIENCE	OCEAN	JAMES
ROCKET	LINGERLE	MUSIC	ATTIC	LIZA
DICEY	BOSTON	FREE SPACE	JOHN	READ
CRISFIELD	MAYBETH	MARBLES	GRAM	HONKY
MILLIE	WELFARE	MINA	CHAPPELLE	APRON

Dicey's Song

SPOON	BOAT	TEN	MONEY	ANGEL
SAMMY	FAT	NOTE	MULBERRY	BOX
GROCERY	ADOPTION	FREE SPACE	SEVEN	THIRTEEN
JEFF	BOOTLEGGING	VOIGT	APRON	CHAPPELLE
MINA	WELFARE	MILLIE	HONKY	GRAM

Dicey's Song

MILLIE	ANGEL	MARBLES	ADOPTION	ROCKET
SAILBOAT	JEFF	MINA	TEN	BOOTLEGGING
OCEAN	THIRTEEN	FREE SPACE	DICEY	BOAT
FAT	BOX	MAYBETH	LIZA	GROCERY
JOHN	SEVEN	MULBERRY	MUSIC	VOIGT

Dicey's Song

WELFARE	READ	SPOON	SCIENCE	JAMES
CRISFIELD	ATTIC	CHAPPELLE	ESSAY	BOSTON
HONKY	APRON	FREE SPACE	MONEY	GRAM
GUITAR	NOTE	LINGERLE	VOIGT	MUSIC
MULBERRY	SEVEN	JOHN	GROCERY	LIZA

Dicey's Song

TEN	MUSIC	GROCERY	DICEY	MILLIE
GUITAR	BOOTLEGGING	FAT	LIZA	SAILBOAT
APRON	HONKY	FREE SPACE	MONEY	SCIENCE
OCEAN	BOAT	SEVEN	ADOPTION	MARBLES
THIRTEEN	MINA	ANGEL	ESSAY	ATTIC

Dicey's Song

WELFARE	JAMES	GRAM	SAMMY	ROCKET
NOTE	MULBERRY	EVERSLEIGH	READ	CRISFIELD
CHAPPELLE	LINGERLE	FREE SPACE	VOIGT	JOHN
JEFF	BOSTON	BOX	ATTIC	ESSAY
ANGEL	MINA	THIRTEEN	MARBLES	ADOPTION

Dicey's Song

BOSTON	MONEY	MILLIE	BOAT	HONKY
MULBERRY	JAMES	DICEY	CRISFIELD	SCIENCE
LIZA	CHAPPELLE	FREE SPACE	ESSAY	SPOON
ADOPTION	ATTIC	EVERSLEIGH	SAILBOAT	WELFARE
ANGEL	READ	JOHN	MUSIC	SAMMY

Dicey's Song

BOOTLEGGING	MINA	FAT	SEVEN	GUITAR
BOX	JEFF	OCEAN	LINGERLE	MARBLES
GRAM	NOTE	FREE SPACE	MAYBETH	VOIGT
THIRTEEN	TEN	GROCERY	SAMMY	MUSIC
JOHN	READ	ANGEL	WELFARE	SAILBOAT

Dicey's Song

HONKY	MAYBETH	MARBLES	GRAM	BOOTLEGGING
MONEY	ROCKET	APRON	EVERSLEIGH	BOAT
GROCERY	WELFARE	FREE SPACE	CRISFIELD	JAMES
ESSAY	MULBERRY	VOIGT	BOSTON	ADOPTION
READ	NOTE	SCIENCE	JEFF	SPOON

Dicey's Song

JOHN	TEN	FAT	THIRTEEN	LIZA
OCEAN	LINGERLE	BOX	DICEY	SAILBOAT
GUITAR	ATTIC	FREE SPACE	MINA	ANGEL
MUSIC	SEVEN	SAMMY	SPOON	JEFF
SCIENCE	NOTE	READ	ADOPTION	BOSTON

Dicey's Song

JEFF	BOSTON	BOOTLEGGING	MAYBETH	EVERSLEIGH
ADOPTION	JOHN	MINA	APRON	SCIENCE
ESSAY	WELFARE	FREE SPACE	LINGERLE	DICEY
SPOON	READ	ATTIC	SEVEN	CRISFIELD
MULBERRY	GROCERY	CHAPPELLE	ANGEL	JAMES

Dicey's Song

HONKY	MUSIC	OCEAN	GUITAR	SAMMY
ROCKET	MONEY	MARBLES	BOAT	THIRTEEN
FAT	SAILBOAT	FREE SPACE	NOTE	TEN
LIZA	MILLIE	BOX	JAMES	ANGEL
CHAPPELLE	GROCERY	MULBERRY	CRISFIELD	SEVEN

Dicey's Song

ANGEL	ADOPTION	BOSTON	BOAT	CRISFIELD
MUSIC	DICEY	BOOTLEGGING	GROCERY	MONEY
SAILBOAT	OCEAN	FREE SPACE	FAT	CHAPPELLE
ATTIC	NOTE	VOIGT	SEVEN	JAMES
MILLIE	GUITAR	JEFF	EVERSLEIGH	MAYBETH

Dicey's Song

MULBERRY	JOHN	MARBLES	SPOON	SCIENCE
SAMMY	LINGERLE	LIZA	TEN	ROCKET
READ	HONKY	FREE SPACE	BOX	WELFARE
THIRTEEN	MINA	ESSAY	MAYBETH	EVERSLEIGH
JEFF	GUITAR	MILLIE	JAMES	SEVEN

Dicey's Song

MINA	DICEY	CRISFIELD	FAT	JAMES
MARBLES	NOTE	BOSTON	GRAM	READ
MULBERRY	OCEAN	FREE SPACE	CHAPPELLE	ANGEL
SEVEN	VOIGT	ROCKET	MUSIC	BOOTLEGGING
BOX	ATTIC	ADOPTION	JOHN	MAYBETH

Dicey's Song

WELFARE	GUITAR	ESSAY	JEFF	SAILBOAT
LINGERLE	MILLIE	SAMMY	MONEY	APRON
THIRTEEN	HONKY	FREE SPACE	SPOON	SCIENCE
LIZA	GROCERY	BOAT	MAYBETH	JOHN
ADOPTION	ATTIC	BOX	BOOTLEGGING	MUSIC

Dicey's Song

TEN	GROCERY	ADOPTION	EVERSLEIGH	BOAT
MARBLES	SPOON	OCEAN	SEVEN	BOSTON
ATTIC	WELFARE	FREE SPACE	JAMES	LIZA
SCIENCE	ESSAY	BOOTLEGGING	MAYBETH	CRISFIELD
JOHN	MONEY	MULBERRY	ROCKET	CHAPPELLE

Dicey's Song

MINA	MUSIC	JEFF	HONKY	VOIGT
NOTE	SAILBOAT	GUITAR	LINGERLE	FAT
APRON	SAMMY	FREE SPACE	ANGEL	THIRTEEN
GRAM	MILLIE	READ	CHAPPELLE	ROCKET
MULBERRY	MONEY	JOHN	CRISFIELD	MAYBETH

Dicey's Song

BOX	SEVEN	HONKY	JOHN	MINA
OCEAN	EVERSLEIGH	ADOPTION	SAILBOAT	VOIGT
MAYBETH	DICEY	FREE SPACE	NOTE	LINGERLE
LIZA	BOAT	FAT	GROCERY	GRAM
CHAPPELLE	GUITAR	THIRTEEN	JAMES	WELFARE

Dicey's Song

ATTIC	JEFF	ANGEL	APRON	BOSTON
CRISFIELD	READ	MILLIE	SAMMY	MARBLES
BOOTLEGGING	MULBERRY	FREE SPACE	ESSAY	SPOON
MONEY	SCIENCE	TEN	WELFARE	JAMES
THIRTEEN	GUITAR	CHAPPELLE	GRAM	GROCERY

Dicey's Song

SPOON	BOSTON	GRAM	READ	EVERSLEIGH
DICEY	SCIENCE	SAMMY	MILLIE	THIRTEEN
MARBLES	SEVEN	FREE SPACE	MINA	APRON
GROCERY	OCEAN	LIZA	ATTIC	TEN
WELFARE	ROCKET	MULBERRY	NOTE	CHAPPELLE

Dicey's Song

MONEY	ANGEL	SAILBOAT	MAYBETH	CRISFIELD
VOIGT	JAMES	ESSAY	LINGERLE	ADOPTION
BOAT	HONKY	FREE SPACE	GUITAR	MUSIC
JEFF	FAT	BOX	CHAPPELLE	NOTE
MULBERRY	ROCKET	WELFARE	TEN	ATTIC

Dicey's Song

LINGERLE	ADOPTION	SAILBOAT	ANGEL	MULBERRY
SEVEN	FAT	DICEY	GROCERY	ROCKET
SAMMY	BOOTLEGGING	FREE SPACE	BOX	EVERSLEIGH
ATTIC	MILLIE	APRON	LIZA	MINA
WELFARE	OCEAN	TEN	MUSIC	MARBLES

Dicey's Song

THIRTEEN	JEFF	ESSAY	NOTE	JAMES
VOIGT	BOSTON	GUITAR	GRAM	CHAPPELLE
MONEY	MAYBETH	FREE SPACE	SPOON	BOAT
READ	SCIENCE	CRISFIELD	MARBLES	MUSIC
TEN	OCEAN	WELFARE	MINA	LIZA

Dicey's Song

ADOPTION	TEN	OCEAN	BOAT	GROCERY
MINA	JEFF	APRON	MILLIE	SAMMY
EVERSLEIGH	CHAPPELLE	FREE SPACE	MULBERRY	HONKY
DICEY	GUITAR	WELFARE	NOTE	MUSIC
LINGERLE	ESSAY	THIRTEEN	JOHN	VOIGT

Dicey's Song

JAMES	MONEY	SEVEN	CRISFIELD	SAILBOAT
BOOTLEGGING	ROCKET	BOSTON	READ	GRAM
ATTIC	LIZA	FREE SPACE	FAT	SCIENCE
ANGEL	MAYBETH	BOX	VOIGT	JOHN
THIRTEEN	ESSAY	LINGERLE	MUSIC	NOTE

Dicey's Song

SAMMY	LINGERLE	MULBERRY	GROCERY	CHAPPELLE
JOHN	MUSIC	HONKY	TEN	MILLIE
CRISFIELD	SAILBOAT	FREE SPACE	JEFF	MAYBETH
ANGEL	READ	ROCKET	FAT	SPOON
MONEY	ESSAY	VOIGT	BOSTON	OCEAN

Dicey's Song

BOOTLEGGING	ADOPTION	MARBLES	MINA	BOAT
APRON	DICEY	SCIENCE	NOTE	EVERSLEIGH
LIZA	WELFARE	FREE SPACE	ATTIC	GRAM
JAMES	SEVEN	BOX	OCEAN	BOSTON
VOIGT	ESSAY	MONEY	SPOON	FAT

Dicey's Song

MUSIC	MULBERRY	LINGERLE	MILLIE	ROCKET
SPOON	SAMMY	CRISFIELD	SCIENCE	APRON
DICEY	LIZA	FREE SPACE	BOX	ANGEL
MONEY	EVERSLEIGH	WELFARE	JAMES	ATTIC
GRAM	SAILBOAT	TEN	CHAPPELLE	NOTE

Dicey's Song

MINA	THIRTEEN	FAT	JEFF	MARBLES
BOOTLEGGING	GROCERY	READ	GUITAR	SEVEN
OCEAN	HONKY	FREE SPACE	ADOPTION	JOHN
ESSAY	VOIGT	BOSTON	NOTE	CHAPPELLE
TEN	SAILBOAT	GRAM	ATTIC	JAMES

Dicey's Song

ATTIC	ESSAY	SEVEN	ROCKET	NOTE
JAMES	BOX	ADOPTION	BOOTLEGGING	EVERSLEIGH
APRON	MULBERRY	FREE SPACE	JOHN	MAYBETH
MINA	WELFARE	MONEY	FAT	DICEY
VOIGT	MILLIE	SCIENCE	JEFF	CHAPPELLE

Dicey's Song

LINGERLE	TEN	CRISFIELD	SAILBOAT	BOSTON
READ	LIZA	THIRTEEN	GROCERY	HONKY
SPOON	GRAM	FREE SPACE	MARBLES	ANGEL
SAMMY	MUSIC	OCEAN	CHAPPELLE	JEFF
SCIENCE	MILLIE	VOIGT	DICEY	FAT

Dicey's Song Vocabulary Word List

No.	Word	Clue/Definition
1.	ANTICIPATING	Looking forward to or expecting
2.	AUREOLE	A radiance encircling the head or body; a halo
3.	BALMY	Soothing; mild; pleasant
4.	CHARISMA	A special quality that inspires allegiance and devotion
5.	CHASTENED	Subdued; restrained from excess
6.	CONFER	To have a conference or talk
7.	CONGEALED	Coagulated; solidified or thickened
8.	CONTRADICT	Oppose verbally; go against; assert the opposite
9.	CONVENIENT	Easy to do, use, or get to
10.	CREMATED	Burnt up; burned a dead body to ashes
11.	DECEITFULNESS	Dishonest action or trick; fraud or lie
12.	DIMINISHED	Made smaller; lessened; reduced
13.	DUMBFOUNDED	Made speechless by shocking; amazed
14.	EMANATE	To flow out; come forth; emit
15.	ENTHUSIASM	Intense or eager interest; passion
16.	FLUENTLY	Write or speak easily, smoothly and expressively
17.	HARRIED	Tormented or worried; harassed
18.	INSISTED	To declare firmly and persistently
19.	INTERFERE	Meddle; hinder; prevent; intervene
20.	INTRUSION	An invasion of privacy
21.	LADEN	Loaded; burdened
22.	LAPEL	Part of a jacket folded back from the neckline
23.	LINGERED	Continued to stay; delayed; loitered
24.	LURCHING	Rolling, pitching or swaying suddenly
25.	MANNIKIN	Models of the human body usually used in stores
26.	MEANDERING	An aimless wandering; rambling
27.	MINSTREL	A traveling poet, singer or musician
28.	MINUET	A slow, stately dance or music for such a dance
29.	MISCHIEF	Teasing; prank; naughty or troublesome act
30.	OPTIMISTIC	Expect the best outcome
31.	PRECISELY	Particularly; exactly
32.	REVERBERATED	To be reflected as light or sound waves
33.	RICKETY	Liable to fall or break down because of weakness
34.	SULKY	Showing resentment and ill humor
35.	SYMMETRICAL	Exact correspondence of form on opposite sides of a dividing line
36.	TENDENCY	Inclination to move or act in a particular way
37.	TRIUMPHANTLY	Successfully; elated
38.	VAGUELY	Not sharp or certain; hazily
39.	WARY	Cautious

Dicey's Song Vocabulary Fill In The Blanks 1

1. Showing resentment and ill humor
2. To flow out; come forth; emit
3. Made smaller; lessened; reduced
4. A radiance encircling the head or body; a halo
5. Rolling, pitching or swaying suddenly
6. Easy to do, use, or get to
7. Loaded; burdened
8. Intense or eager interest; passion
9. Successfully; elated
10. A slow, stately dance or music for such a dance
11. Liable to fall or break down because of weakness
12. Particularly; exactly
13. Burnt up; burned a dead body to ashes
14. Write or speak easily, smoothly and expressively
15. Tormented or worried; harassed
16. Made speechless by shocking; amazed
17. To declare firmly and persistently
18. Looking forward to or expecting
19. Part of a jacket folded back from the neckline
20. A special quality that inspires allegiance and devotion

Dicey's Song Vocabulary Fill In The Blanks 1 Answer Key

SULKY	1. Showing resentment and ill humor
EMANATE	2. To flow out; come forth; emit
DIMINISHED	3. Made smaller; lessened; reduced
AUREOLE	4. A radiance encircling the head or body; a halo
LURCHING	5. Rolling, pitching or swaying suddenly
CONVENIENT	6. Easy to do, use, or get to
LADEN	7. Loaded; burdened
ENTHUSIASM	8. Intense or eager interest; passion
TRIUMPHANTLY	9. Successfully; elated
MINUET	10. A slow, stately dance or music for such a dance
RICKETY	11. Liable to fall or break down because of weakness
PRECISELY	12. Particularly; exactly
CREMATED	13. Burnt up; burned a dead body to ashes
FLUENTLY	14. Write or speak easily, smoothly and expressively
HARRIED	15. Tormented or worried; harassed
DUMBFOUNDED	16. Made speechless by shocking; amazed
INSISTED	17. To declare firmly and persistently
ANTICIPATING	18. Looking forward to or expecting
LAPEL	19. Part of a jacket folded back from the neckline
CHARISMA	20. A special quality that inspires allegiance and devotion

Dicey's Song Vocabulary Fill In The Blanks 2

1. Cautious
2. Loaded; burdened
3. Write or speak easily, smoothly and expressively
4. Made smaller; lessened; reduced
5. Looking forward to or expecting
6. To declare firmly and persistently
7. Exact correspondence of form on opposite sides of a dividing line
8. Teasing; prank; naughty or troublesome act
9. To be reflected as light or sound waves
10. Particularly; exactly
11. Oppose verbally; go against; assert the opposite
12. A radiance encircling the head or body; a halo
13. An invasion of privacy
14. Made speechless by shocking; amazed
15. An aimless wandering; rambling
16. Models of the human body usually used in stores
17. Inclination to move or act in a particular way
18. Soothing; mild; pleasant
19. Tormented or worried; harassed
20. Continued to stay; delayed; loitered

Dicey's Song Vocabulary Fill In The Blanks 2 Answer Key

WARY	1. Cautious
LADEN	2. Loaded; burdened
FLUENTLY	3. Write or speak easily, smoothly and expressively
DIMINISHED	4. Made smaller; lessened; reduced
ANTICIPATING	5. Looking forward to or expecting
INSISTED	6. To declare firmly and persistently
SYMMETRICAL	7. Exact correspondence of form on opposite sides of a dividing line
MISCHIEF	8. Teasing; prank; naughty or troublesome act
REVERBERATED	9. To be reflected as light or sound waves
PRECISELY	10. Particularly; exactly
CONTRADICT	11. Oppose verbally; go against; assert the opposite
AUREOLE	12. A radiance encircling the head or body; a halo
INTRUSION	13. An invasion of privacy
DUMBFOUNDED	14. Made speechless by shocking; amazed
MEANDERING	15. An aimless wandering; rambling
MANNIKIN	16. Models of the human body usually used in stores
TENDENCY	17. Inclination to move or act in a particular way
BALMY	18. Soothing; mild; pleasant
HARRIED	19. Tormented or worried; harassed
LINGERED	20. Continued to stay; delayed; loitered

Dicey's Song Vocabulary Fill In The Blanks 3

1. Easy to do, use, or get to
2. Tormented or worried; harassed
3. Made speechless by shocking; amazed
4. Not sharp or certain; hazily
5. To flow out; come forth; emit
6. Meddle; hinder; prevent; intervene
7. A slow, stately dance or music for such a dance
8. Coagulated; solidified or thickened
9. Write or speak easily, smoothly and expressively
10. Models of the human body usually used in stores
11. Intense or eager interest; passion
12. A traveling poet, singer or musician
13. Looking forward to or expecting
14. Showing resentment and ill humor
15. A special quality that inspires allegiance and devotion
16. Cautious
17. To be reflected as light or sound waves
18. Rolling, pitching or swaying suddenly
19. Particularly; exactly
20. Burnt up; burned a dead body to ashes

Dicey's Song Vocabulary Fill In The Blanks 3 Answer Key

CONVENIENT	1. Easy to do, use, or get to
HARRIED	2. Tormented or worried; harassed
DUMBFOUNDED	3. Made speechless by shocking; amazed
VAGUELY	4. Not sharp or certain; hazily
EMANATE	5. To flow out; come forth; emit
INTERFERE	6. Meddle; hinder; prevent; intervene
MINUET	7. A slow, stately dance or music for such a dance
CONGEALED	8. Coagulated; solidified or thickened
FLUENTLY	9. Write or speak easily, smoothly and expressively
MANNIKIN	10. Models of the human body usually used in stores
ENTHUSIASM	11. Intense or eager interest; passion
MINSTREL	12. A traveling poet, singer or musician
ANTICIPATING	13. Looking forward to or expecting
SULKY	14. Showing resentment and ill humor
CHARISMA	15. A special quality that inspires allegiance and devotion
WARY	16. Cautious
REVERBERATED	17. To be reflected as light or sound waves
LURCHING	18. Rolling, pitching or swaying suddenly
PRECISELY	19. Particularly; exactly
CREMATED	20. Burnt up; burned a dead body to ashes

Dicey's Song Vocabulary Fill In The Blanks 4

_____ 1. Subdued; restrained from excess

_____ 2. A special quality that inspires allegiance and devotion

_____ 3. Exact correspondence of form on opposite sides of a dividing line

_____ 4. Made smaller; lessened; reduced

_____ 5. Liable to fall or break down because of weakness

_____ 6. Loaded; burdened

_____ 7. Dishonest action or trick; fraud or lie

_____ 8. Coagulated; solidified or thickened

_____ 9. Easy to do, use, or get to

_____ 10. A traveling poet, singer or musician

_____ 11. Soothing; mild; pleasant

_____ 12. Cautious

_____ 13. Particularly; exactly

_____ 14. Tormented or worried; harassed

_____ 15. An invasion of privacy

_____ 16. Expect the best outcome

_____ 17. Continued to stay; delayed; loitered

_____ 18. A slow, stately dance or music for such a dance

_____ 19. To declare firmly and persistently

_____ 20. Part of a jacket folded back from the neckline

Dicey's Song Vocabulary Fill In The Blanks 4 Answer Key

CHASTENED	1. Subdued; restrained from excess
CHARISMA	2. A special quality that inspires allegiance and devotion
SYMMETRICAL	3. Exact correspondence of form on opposite sides of a dividing line
DIMINISHED	4. Made smaller; lessened; reduced
RICKETY	5. Liable to fall or break down because of weakness
LADEN	6. Loaded; burdened
DECEITFULNESS	7. Dishonest action or trick; fraud or lie
CONGEALED	8. Coagulated; solidified or thickened
CONVENIENT	9. Easy to do, use, or get to
MINSTREL	10. A traveling poet, singer or musician
BALMY	11. Soothing; mild; pleasant
WARY	12. Cautious
PRECISELY	13. Particularly; exactly
HARRIED	14. Tormented or worried; harassed
INTRUSION	15. An invasion of privacy
OPTIMISTIC	16. Expect the best outcome
LINGERED	17. Continued to stay; delayed; loitered
MINUET	18. A slow, stately dance or music for such a dance
INSISTED	19. To declare firmly and persistently
LAPEL	20. Part of a jacket folded back from the neckline

Dicey's Song Vocabulary Matching 1

___ 1. WARY A. Loaded; burdened
___ 2. CREMATED B. To be reflected as light or sound waves
___ 3. PRECISELY C. Successfully; elated
___ 4. MEANDERING D. A radiance encircling the head or body; a halo
___ 5. TENDENCY E. An aimless wandering; rambling
___ 6. MISCHIEF F. To declare firmly and persistently
___ 7. VAGUELY G. Burnt up; burned a dead body to ashes
___ 8. AUREOLE H. Soothing; mild; pleasant
___ 9. SULKY I. Cautious
___ 10. MINSTREL J. Oppose verbally; go against; assert the opposite
___ 11. DUMBFOUNDED K. Intense or eager interest; passion
___ 12. CONGEALED L. Inclination to move or act in a particular way
___ 13. INSISTED M. Tormented or worried; harassed
___ 14. CONTRADICT N. An invasion of privacy
___ 15. HARRIED O. Showing resentment and ill humor
___ 16. CHASTENED P. Coagulated; solidified or thickened
___ 17. REVERBERATED Q. Made speechless by shocking; amazed
___ 18. INTRUSION R. Subdued; restrained from excess
___ 19. ENTHUSIASM S. Liable to fall or break down because of weakness
___ 20. LADEN T. Not sharp or certain; hazily
___ 21. TRIUMPHANTLY U. A traveling poet, singer or musician
___ 22. ANTICIPATING V. Looking forward to or expecting
___ 23. RICKETY W. Teasing; prank; naughty or troublesome act
___ 24. BALMY X. Write or speak easily, smoothly and expressively
___ 25. FLUENTLY Y. Particularly; exactly

Dicey's Song Vocabulary Matching 1 Answer Key

I - 1.	WARY	A. Loaded; burdened
G - 2.	CREMATED	B. To be reflected as light or sound waves
Y - 3.	PRECISELY	C. Successfully; elated
E - 4.	MEANDERING	D. A radiance encircling the head or body; a halo
L - 5.	TENDENCY	E. An aimless wandering; rambling
W - 6.	MISCHIEF	F. To declare firmly and persistently
T - 7.	VAGUELY	G. Burnt up; burned a dead body to ashes
D - 8.	AUREOLE	H. Soothing; mild; pleasant
O - 9.	SULKY	I. Cautious
U - 10.	MINSTREL	J. Oppose verbally; go against; assert the opposite
Q - 11.	DUMBFOUNDED	K. Intense or eager interest; passion
P - 12.	CONGEALED	L. Inclination to move or act in a particular way
F - 13.	INSISTED	M. Tormented or worried; harassed
J - 14.	CONTRADICT	N. An invasion of privacy
M - 15.	HARRIED	O. Showing resentment and ill humor
R - 16.	CHASTENED	P. Coagulated; solidified or thickened
B - 17.	REVERBERATED	Q. Made speechless by shocking; amazed
N - 18.	INTRUSION	R. Subdued; restrained from excess
K - 19.	ENTHUSIASM	S. Liable to fall or break down because of weakness
A - 20.	LADEN	T. Not sharp or certain; hazily
C - 21.	TRIUMPHANTLY	U. A traveling poet, singer or musician
V - 22.	ANTICIPATING	V. Looking forward to or expecting
S - 23.	RICKETY	W. Teasing; prank; naughty or troublesome act
H - 24.	BALMY	X. Write or speak easily, smoothly and expressively
X - 25.	FLUENTLY	Y. Particularly; exactly

Copyrighted

Dicey's Song Vocabulary Matching 2

___ 1. OPTIMISTIC   A. Easy to do, use, or get to
___ 2. VAGUELY   B. A special quality that inspires allegiance and devotion
___ 3. LINGERED   C. Liable to fall or break down because of weakness
___ 4. SULKY   D. A traveling poet, singer or musician
___ 5. WARY   E. Dishonest action or trick; fraud or lie
___ 6. DECEITFULNESS   F. Coagulated; solidified or thickened
___ 7. ANTICIPATING   G. Made smaller; lessened; reduced
___ 8. BALMY   H. Continued to stay; delayed; loitered
___ 9. HARRIED   I. Soothing; mild; pleasant
___ 10. FLUENTLY   J. Tormented or worried; harassed
___ 11. CHARISMA   K. Burnt up; burned a dead body to ashes
___ 12. MINSTREL   L. Write or speak easily, smoothly and expressively
___ 13. CONVENIENT   M. Looking forward to or expecting
___ 14. AUREOLE   N. Expect the best outcome
___ 15. MANNIKIN   O. Inclination to move or act in a particular way
___ 16. PRECISELY   P. Showing resentment and ill humor
___ 17. RICKETY   Q. Not sharp or certain; hazily
___ 18. ENTHUSIASM   R. A radiance encircling the head or body; a halo
___ 19. CREMATED   S. An aimless wandering; rambling
___ 20. INSISTED   T. Models of the human body usually used in stores
___ 21. MINUET   U. To declare firmly and persistently
___ 22. DIMINISHED   V. Intense or eager interest; passion
___ 23. MEANDERING   W. Cautious
___ 24. CONGEALED   X. Particularly; exactly
___ 25. TENDENCY   Y. A slow, stately dance or music for such a dance

Dicey's Song Vocabulary Matching 2 Answer Key

N - 1. OPTIMISTIC		A. Easy to do, use, or get to
Q - 2. VAGUELY		B. A special quality that inspires allegiance and devotion
H - 3. LINGERED		C. Liable to fall or break down because of weakness
P - 4. SULKY		D. A traveling poet, singer or musician
W - 5. WARY		E. Dishonest action or trick; fraud or lie
E - 6. DECEITFULNESS		F. Coagulated; solidified or thickened
M - 7. ANTICIPATING		G. Made smaller; lessened; reduced
I - 8. BALMY		H. Continued to stay; delayed; loitered
J - 9. HARRIED		I. Soothing; mild; pleasant
L - 10. FLUENTLY		J. Tormented or worried; harassed
B - 11. CHARISMA		K. Burnt up; burned a dead body to ashes
D - 12. MINSTREL		L. Write or speak easily, smoothly and expressively
A - 13. CONVENIENT		M. Looking forward to or expecting
R - 14. AUREOLE		N. Expect the best outcome
T - 15. MANNIKIN		O. Inclination to move or act in a particular way
X - 16. PRECISELY		P. Showing resentment and ill humor
C - 17. RICKETY		Q. Not sharp or certain; hazily
V - 18. ENTHUSIASM		R. A radiance encircling the head or body; a halo
K - 19. CREMATED		S. An aimless wandering; rambling
U - 20. INSISTED		T. Models of the human body usually used in stores
Y - 21. MINUET		U. To declare firmly and persistently
G - 22. DIMINISHED		V. Intense or eager interest; passion
S - 23. MEANDERING		W. Cautious
F - 24. CONGEALED		X. Particularly; exactly
O - 25. TENDENCY		Y. A slow, stately dance or music for such a dance

Dicey's Song Vocabulary Matching 3

___ 1. ENTHUSIASM   A. Meddle; hinder; prevent; intervene
___ 2. INSISTED   B. Intense or eager interest; passion
___ 3. CONTRADICT   C. Part of a jacket folded back from the neckline
___ 4. PRECISELY   D. Liable to fall or break down because of weakness
___ 5. FLUENTLY   E. An invasion of privacy
___ 6. WARY   F. Coagulated; solidified or thickened
___ 7. AUREOLE   G. To have a conference or talk
___ 8. CONGEALED   H. Cautious
___ 9. ANTICIPATING   I. Expect the best outcome
___ 10. CONVENIENT   J. Easy to do, use, or get to
___ 11. LAPEL   K. Particularly; exactly
___ 12. TENDENCY   L. Successfully; elated
___ 13. DUMBFOUNDED   M. Made speechless by shocking; amazed
___ 14. CHASTENED   N. A radiance encircling the head or body; a halo
___ 15. TRIUMPHANTLY   O. Subdued; restrained from excess
___ 16. BALMY   P. A slow, stately dance or music for such a dance
___ 17. CONFER   Q. Soothing; mild; pleasant
___ 18. RICKETY   R. A special quality that inspires allegiance and devotion
___ 19. MINUET   S. To declare firmly and persistently
___ 20. CHARISMA   T. Oppose verbally; go against; assert the opposite
___ 21. MANNIKIN   U. Write or speak easily, smoothly and expressively
___ 22. OPTIMISTIC   V. Continued to stay; delayed; loitered
___ 23. INTRUSION   W. Looking forward to or expecting
___ 24. INTERFERE   X. Inclination to move or act in a particular way
___ 25. LINGERED   Y. Models of the human body usually used in stores

Dicey's Song Vocabulary Matching 3 Answer Key

B - 1. ENTHUSIASM	A. Meddle; hinder; prevent; intervene
S - 2. INSISTED	B. Intense or eager interest; passion
T - 3. CONTRADICT	C. Part of a jacket folded back from the neckline
K - 4. PRECISELY	D. Liable to fall or break down because of weakness
U - 5. FLUENTLY	E. An invasion of privacy
H - 6. WARY	F. Coagulated; solidified or thickened
N - 7. AUREOLE	G. To have a conference or talk
F - 8. CONGEALED	H. Cautious
W - 9. ANTICIPATING	I. Expect the best outcome
J - 10. CONVENIENT	J. Easy to do, use, or get to
C - 11. LAPEL	K. Particularly; exactly
X - 12. TENDENCY	L. Successfully; elated
M - 13. DUMBFOUNDED	M. Made speechless by shocking; amazed
O - 14. CHASTENED	N. A radiance encircling the head or body; a halo
L - 15. TRIUMPHANTLY	O. Subdued; restrained from excess
Q - 16. BALMY	P. A slow, stately dance or music for such a dance
G - 17. CONFER	Q. Soothing; mild; pleasant
D - 18. RICKETY	R. A special quality that inspires allegiance and devotion
P - 19. MINUET	S. To declare firmly and persistently
R - 20. CHARISMA	T. Oppose verbally; go against; assert the opposite
Y - 21. MANNIKIN	U. Write or speak easily, smoothly and expressively
I - 22. OPTIMISTIC	V. Continued to stay; delayed; loitered
E - 23. INTRUSION	W. Looking forward to or expecting
A - 24. INTERFERE	X. Inclination to move or act in a particular way
V - 25. LINGERED	Y. Models of the human body usually used in stores

Dicey's Song Vocabulary Matching 4

____ 1. CHARISMA   A. An invasion of privacy
____ 2. VAGUELY   B. Continued to stay; delayed; loitered
____ 3. MEANDERING   C. A radiance encircling the head or body; a halo
____ 4. CONTRADICT   D. Cautious
____ 5. ANTICIPATING   E. An aimless wandering; rambling
____ 6. AUREOLE   F. Made speechless by shocking; amazed
____ 7. INTRUSION   G. Looking forward to or expecting
____ 8. TENDENCY   H. To be reflected as light or sound waves
____ 9. TRIUMPHANTLY   I. A slow, stately dance or music for such a dance
____10. LAPEL   J. Showing resentment and ill humor
____11. LINGERED   K. A special quality that inspires allegiance and devotion
____12. MINUET   L. Subdued; restrained from excess
____13. WARY   M. Loaded; burdened
____14. REVERBERATED   N. Teasing; prank; naughty or troublesome act
____15. MANNIKIN   O. Rolling, pitching or swaying suddenly
____16. BALMY   P. Part of a jacket folded back from the neckline
____17. LADEN   Q. Not sharp or certain; hazily
____18. CONVENIENT   R. To have a conference or talk
____19. CONGEALED   S. Oppose verbally; go against; assert the opposite
____20. CONFER   T. Successfully; elated
____21. SULKY   U. Easy to do, use, or get to
____22. LURCHING   V. Models of the human body usually used in stores
____23. CHASTENED   W. Coagulated; solidified or thickened
____24. MISCHIEF   X. Soothing; mild; pleasant
____25. DUMBFOUNDED   Y. Inclination to move or act in a particular way

Dicey's Song Vocabulary Matching 4 Answer Key

K - 1. CHARISMA	A. An invasion of privacy
Q - 2. VAGUELY	B. Continued to stay; delayed; loitered
E - 3. MEANDERING	C. A radiance encircling the head or body; a halo
S - 4. CONTRADICT	D. Cautious
G - 5. ANTICIPATING	E. An aimless wandering; rambling
C - 6. AUREOLE	F. Made speechless by shocking; amazed
A - 7. INTRUSION	G. Looking forward to or expecting
Y - 8. TENDENCY	H. To be reflected as light or sound waves
T - 9. TRIUMPHANTLY	I. A slow, stately dance or music for such a dance
P - 10. LAPEL	J. Showing resentment and ill humor
B - 11. LINGERED	K. A special quality that inspires allegiance and devotion
I - 12. MINUET	L. Subdued; restrained from excess
D - 13. WARY	M. Loaded; burdened
H - 14. REVERBERATED	N. Teasing; prank; naughty or troublesome act
V - 15. MANNIKIN	O. Rolling, pitching or swaying suddenly
X - 16. BALMY	P. Part of a jacket folded back from the neckline
M - 17. LADEN	Q. Not sharp or certain; hazily
U - 18. CONVENIENT	R. To have a conference or talk
W - 19. CONGEALED	S. Oppose verbally; go against; assert the opposite
R - 20. CONFER	T. Successfully; elated
J - 21. SULKY	U. Easy to do, use, or get to
O - 22. LURCHING	V. Models of the human body usually used in stores
L - 23. CHASTENED	W. Coagulated; solidified or thickened
N - 24. MISCHIEF	X. Soothing; mild; pleasant
F - 25. DUMBFOUNDED	Y. Inclination to move or act in a particular way

Dicey's Song Vocabulary Magic Squares 1

Match the definition with the vocabulary word. Put your answers in the magic squares below. When your answers are correct, all columns and rows will add to the same number.

A. HARRIED
B. AUREOLE
C. LINGERED
D. PRECISELY
E. CONFER
F. CONTRADICT
G. SULKY
H. TENDENCY
I. MINUET
J. MEANDERING
K. LAPEL
L. LURCHING
M. INSISTED
N. RICKETY
O. MINSTREL
P. OPTIMISTIC

1. Oppose verbally; go against; assert the opposite
2. A slow, stately dance or music for such a dance
3. A traveling poet, singer or musician
4. Particularly; exactly
5. To declare firmly and persistently
6. A radiance encircling the head or body; a halo
7. Inclination to move or act in a particular way
8. Part of a jacket folded back from the neckline
9. Continued to stay; delayed; loitered
10. Expect the best outcome
11. An aimless wandering; rambling
12. To have a conference or talk
13. Rolling, pitching or swaying suddenly
14. Showing resentment and ill humor
15. Tormented or worried; harassed
16. Liable to fall or break down because of weakness

A=	B=	C=	D=
E=	F=	G=	H=
I=	J=	K=	L=
M=	N=	O=	P=

Dicey's Song Vocabulary Magic Squares 1 Answer Key

Match the definition with the vocabulary word. Put your answers in the magic squares below. When your answers are correct, all columns and rows will add to the same number.

A. HARRIED
B. AUREOLE
C. LINGERED
D. PRECISELY
E. CONFER
F. CONTRADICT
G. SULKY
H. TENDENCY
I. MINUET
J. MEANDERING
K. LAPEL
L. LURCHING
M. INSISTED
N. RICKETY
O. MINSTREL
P. OPTIMISTIC

1. Oppose verbally; go against; assert the opposite
2. A slow, stately dance or music for such a dance
3. A traveling poet, singer or musician
4. Particularly; exactly
5. To declare firmly and persistently
6. A radiance encircling the head or body; a halo
7. Inclination to move or act in a particular way
8. Part of a jacket folded back from the neckline
9. Continued to stay; delayed; loitered
10. Expect the best outcome
11. An aimless wandering; rambling
12. To have a conference or talk
13. Rolling, pitching or swaying suddenly
14. Showing resentment and ill humor
15. Tormented or worried; harassed
16. Liable to fall or break down because of weakness

A=15	B=6	C=9	D=4
E=12	F=1	G=14	H=7
I=2	J=11	K=8	L=13
M=5	N=16	O=3	P=10

Dicey's Song Vocabulary Magic Squares 2

Match the definition with the vocabulary word. Put your answers in the magic squares below. When your answers are correct, all columns and rows will add to the same number.

A. LURCHING
B. DUMBFOUNDED
C. DIMINISHED
D. CONFER
E. CHARISMA
F. LINGERED
G. AUREOLE
H. WARY
I. FLUENTLY
J. PRECISELY
K. MISCHIEF
L. DECEITFULNESS
M. BALMY
N. CONGEALED
O. VAGUELY
P. INSISTED

1. Cautious
2. Soothing; mild; pleasant
3. Made speechless by shocking; amazed
4. Teasing; prank; naughty or troublesome act
5. Particularly; exactly
6. Made smaller; lessened; reduced
7. To declare firmly and persistently
8. A special quality that inspires allegiance and devotion
9. Not sharp or certain; hazily
10. Continued to stay; delayed; loitered
11. Write or speak easily, smoothly and expressively
12. To have a conference or talk
13. Rolling, pitching or swaying suddenly
14. Dishonest action or trick; fraud or lie
15. A radiance encircling the head or body; a halo
16. Coagulated; solidified or thickened

A=	B=	C=	D=
E=	F=	G=	H=
I=	J=	K=	L=
M=	N=	O=	P=

Dicey's Song Vocabulary Magic Squares 2 Answer Key

Match the definition with the vocabulary word. Put your answers in the magic squares below. When your answers are correct, all columns and rows will add to the same number.

A. LURCHING
B. DUMBFOUNDED
C. DIMINISHED
D. CONFER
E. CHARISMA
F. LINGERED
G. AUREOLE
H. WARY
I. FLUENTLY
J. PRECISELY
K. MISCHIEF
L. DECEITFULNESS
M. BALMY
N. CONGEALED
O. VAGUELY
P. INSISTED

1. Cautious
2. Soothing; mild; pleasant
3. Made speechless by shocking; amazed
4. Teasing; prank; naughty or troublesome act
5. Particularly; exactly
6. Made smaller; lessened; reduced
7. To declare firmly and persistently
8. A special quality that inspires allegiance and devotion
9. Not sharp or certain; hazily
10. Continued to stay; delayed; loitered
11. Write or speak easily, smoothly and expressively
12. To have a conference or talk
13. Rolling, pitching or swaying suddenly
14. Dishonest action or trick; fraud or lie
15. A radiance encircling the head or body; a halo
16. Coagulated; solidified or thickened

A=13	B=3	C=6	D=12
E=8	F=10	G=15	H=1
I=11	J=5	K=4	L=14
M=2	N=16	O=9	P=7

Dicey's Song Vocabulary Magic Squares 3

Match the definition with the vocabulary word. Put your answers in the magic squares below. When your answers are correct, all columns and rows will add to the same number.

A. MANNIKIN
B. MINSTREL
C. SULKY
D. RICKETY
E. CONVENIENT
F. PRECISELY
G. TENDENCY
H. REVERBERATED
I. AUREOLE
J. EMANATE
K. MEANDERING
L. INSISTED
M. DIMINISHED
N. LAPEL
O. LINGERED
P. LADEN

1. Part of a jacket folded back from the neckline
2. Inclination to move or act in a particular way
3. To declare firmly and persistently
4. Models of the human body usually used in stores
5. An aimless wandering; rambling
6. A traveling poet, singer or musician
7. Made smaller; lessened; reduced
8. To be reflected as light or sound waves
9. Easy to do, use, or get to
10. Loaded; burdened
11. Showing resentment and ill humor
12. To flow out; come forth; emit
13. Liable to fall or break down because of weakness
14. A radiance encircling the head or body; a halo
15. Particularly; exactly
16. Continued to stay; delayed; loitered

A=	B=	C=	D=
E=	F=	G=	H=
I=	J=	K=	L=
M=	N=	O=	P=

Dicey's Song Vocabulary Magic Squares 3 Answer Key

Match the definition with the vocabulary word. Put your answers in the magic squares below. When your answers are correct, all columns and rows will add to the same number.

A. MANNIKIN
B. MINSTREL
C. SULKY
D. RICKETY
E. CONVENIENT
F. PRECISELY
G. TENDENCY
H. REVERBERATED
I. AUREOLE
J. EMANATE
K. MEANDERING
L. INSISTED
M. DIMINISHED
N. LAPEL
O. LINGERED
P. LADEN

1. Part of a jacket folded back from the neckline
2. Inclination to move or act in a particular way
3. To declare firmly and persistently
4. Models of the human body usually used in stores
5. An aimless wandering; rambling
6. A traveling poet, singer or musician
7. Made smaller; lessened; reduced
8. To be reflected as light or sound waves
9. Easy to do, use, or get to
10. Loaded; burdened
11. Showing resentment and ill humor
12. To flow out; come forth; emit
13. Liable to fall or break down because of weakness
14. A radiance encircling the head or body; a halo
15. Particularly; exactly
16. Continued to stay; delayed; loitered

A=4	B=6	C=11	D=13
E=9	F=15	G=2	H=8
I=14	J=12	K=5	L=3
M=7	N=1	O=16	P=10

Dicey's Song Vocabulary Magic Squares 4

Match the definition with the vocabulary word. Put your answers in the magic squares below. When your answers are correct, all columns and rows will add to the same number.

A. MISCHIEF
B. REVERBERATED
C. AUREOLE
D. SYMMETRICAL
E. INTRUSION
F. DECEITFULNESS
G. SULKY
H. DUMBFOUNDED
I. ENTHUSIASM
J. MINUET
K. TENDENCY
L. CONFER
M. CONVENIENT
N. CHARISMA
O. MINSTREL
P. FLUENTLY

1. Made speechless by shocking; amazed
2. Teasing; prank; naughty or troublesome act
3. To be reflected as light or sound waves
4. Showing resentment and ill humor
5. A slow, stately dance or music for such a dance
6. A traveling poet, singer or musician
7. Write or speak easily, smoothly and expressively
8. Intense or eager interest; passion
9. Inclination to move or act in a particular way
10. A special quality that inspires allegiance and devotion
11. Easy to do, use, or get to
12. To have a conference or talk
13. An invasion of privacy
14. Exact correspondence of form on opposite sides of a dividing line
15. A radiance encircling the head or body; a halo
16. Dishonest action or trick; fraud or lie

A=	B=	C=	D=
E=	F=	G=	H=
I=	J=	K=	L=
M=	N=	O=	P=

Dicey's Song Vocabulary Magic Squares 4 Answer Key

Match the definition with the vocabulary word. Put your answers in the magic squares below. When your answers are correct, all columns and rows will add to the same number.

A. MISCHIEF
B. REVERBERATED
C. AUREOLE
D. SYMMETRICAL
E. INTRUSION
F. DECEITFULNESS
G. SULKY
H. DUMBFOUNDED
I. ENTHUSIASM
J. MINUET
K. TENDENCY
L. CONFER
M. CONVENIENT
N. CHARISMA
O. MINSTREL
P. FLUENTLY

1. Made speechless by shocking; amazed
2. Teasing; prank; naughty or troublesome act
3. To be reflected as light or sound waves
4. Showing resentment and ill humor
5. A slow, stately dance or music for such a dance
6. A traveling poet, singer or musician
7. Write or speak easily, smoothly and expressively
8. Intense or eager interest; passion
9. Inclination to move or act in a particular way
10. A special quality that inspires allegiance and devotion
11. Easy to do, use, or get to
12. To have a conference or talk
13. An invasion of privacy
14. Exact correspondence of form on opposite sides of a dividing line
15. A radiance encircling the head or body; a halo
16. Dishonest action or trick; fraud or lie

A=2	B=3	C=15	D=14
E=13	F=16	G=4	H=1
I=8	J=5	K=9	L=12
M=11	N=10	O=6	P=7

Dicey's Song Vocabulary Word Search 1

Words are placed backwards, forward, diagonally, up and down. Clues listed below can help you find the words. Circle the hidden vocabulary words in the maze.

```
H A X N W D C H A R I S M A T D F Z
L U D E T A N A M E K F N E R E I N
N R B Y Y J R G A V R T U Y I T N L
D E I R R A H Y N T I N M H U S T W
W O N K P X B E N C I L C O M I R J
V L Z T R B D Q I M A S K P P S U C
A E M K H A C P K B I D X T H N S Q
G S W E L U A T I M E Y T I A I I D
U Y C W A T S Z N H C C M M N N O D
E M W R I N D I S S I N I I T T N P
L M L N E B D I A D R E N S L E Y L
Y E G I X M N E A S L D S T Y R D X
M T V N N I A R R E M N T I Y F R J
V R W V M G T T P I P E R C N E I X
J I B I H N E A E X N T E D F R C C
L C D F O G L R R D J G L N C E K S
J A K C H A S T E N E D O B X S E H
M L S U L K Y H Y D T C M Y L V T Z
L U R C H I N G P R E C I S E L Y
```

A radiance encircling the head or body; a halo (7)
A slow, stately dance or music for such a dance (6)
A special quality that inspires allegiance and devotion (8)
A traveling poet, singer or musician (8)
An aimless wandering; rambling (10)
An invasion of privacy (9)
Burnt up; burned a dead body to ashes (8)
Cautious (4)
Continued to stay; delayed; loitered (8)
Exact correspondence of form on opposite sides of a dividing line (11)
Expect the best outcome (10)
Inclination to move or act in a particular way (8)
Intense or eager interest; passion (10)
Liable to fall or break down because of weakness (7)
Loaded; burdened (5)
Looking forward to or expecting (12)

Made smaller; lessened; reduced (10)
Meddle; hinder; prevent; intervene (9)
Models of the human body usually used in stores (8)
Not sharp or certain; hazily (7)
Oppose verbally; go against; assert the opposite (10)
Part of a jacket folded back from the neckline (5)
Particularly; exactly (9)
Rolling, pitching or swaying suddenly (8)
Showing resentment and ill humor (5)
Soothing; mild; pleasant (5)
Subdued; restrained from excess (9)
Successfully; elated (12)
Teasing; prank; naughty or troublesome act (8)
To declare firmly and persistently (8)
To flow out; come forth; emit (7)
To have a conference or talk (6)
Tormented or worried; harassed (7)

Dicey's Song Vocabulary Word Search 1 Answer Key

Words are placed backwards, forward, diagonally, up and down. Clues listed below can help you find the words. Circle the hidden vocabulary words in the maze.

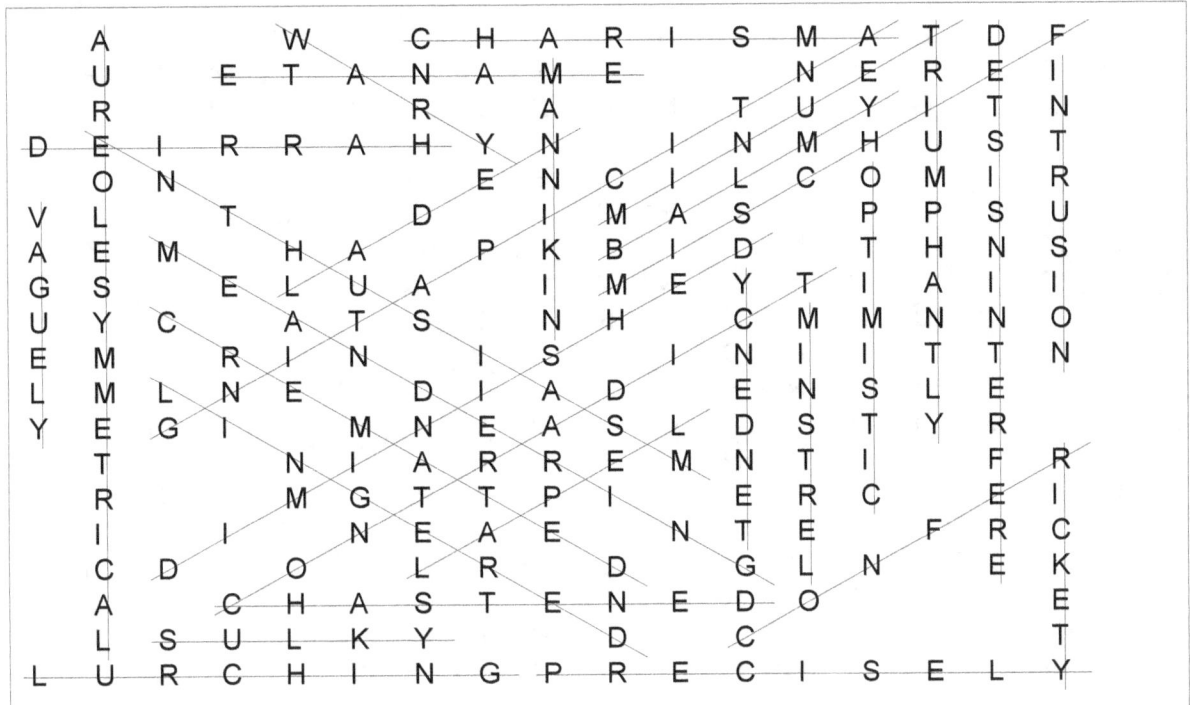

A radiance encircling the head or body; a halo (7)
A slow, stately dance or music for such a dance (6)
A special quality that inspires allegiance and devotion (8)
A traveling poet, singer or musician (8)
An aimless wandering; rambling (10)
An invasion of privacy (9)
Burnt up; burned a dead body to ashes (8)
Cautious (4)
Continued to stay; delayed; loitered (8)
Exact correspondence of form on opposite sides of a dividing line (11)
Expect the best outcome (10)
Inclination to move or act in a particular way (8)
Intense or eager interest; passion (10)
Liable to fall or break down because of weakness (7)
Loaded; burdened (5)
Looking forward to or expecting (12)

Made smaller; lessened; reduced (10)
Meddle; hinder; prevent; intervene (9)
Models of the human body usually used in stores (8)
Not sharp or certain; hazily (7)
Oppose verbally; go against; assert the opposite (10)
Part of a jacket folded back from the neckline (5)
Particularly; exactly (9)
Rolling, pitching or swaying suddenly (8)
Showing resentment and ill humor (5)
Soothing; mild; pleasant (5)
Subdued; restrained from excess (9)
Successfully; elated (12)
Teasing; prank; naughty or troublesome act (8)
To declare firmly and persistently (8)
To flow out; come forth; emit (7)
To have a conference or talk (6)
Tormented or worried; harassed (7)

Dicey's Song Vocabulary Word Search 2

Words are placed backwards, forward, diagonally, up and down. Clues listed below can help you find the words. Circle the hidden vocabulary words in the maze.

C	O	N	V	E	N	I	E	N	T	S	E	T	A	N	A	M	E
P	H	C	L	D	W	W	L	O	Q	Y	U	Q	Y	T	W	I	P
G	R	A	E	G	D	P	O	I	H	M	F	L	F	M	N	N	H
X	Y	Y	R	N	E	Q	E	S	M	M	L	J	K	M	T	U	P
X	T	D	T	I	H	C	R	U	T	E	U	H	A	Y	O	E	Z
Z	E	E	S	H	S	B	U	R	P	T	E	N	S	C	P	T	W
X	K	T	N	C	I	M	A	T	F	R	N	P	E	R	T	R	Z
M	C	S	I	R	N	X	A	N	Y	I	T	K	N	E	I	I	C
V	I	I	M	U	I	H	Z	I	K	C	L	Y	T	M	M	U	W
A	R	S	P	L	M	A	C	I	P	A	Y	J	H	A	I	M	L
G	M	N	C	B	I	R	N	J	Y	L	T	Y	U	T	S	P	D
U	W	I	Z	H	D	R	G	C	L	D	C	L	S	E	T	H	J
E	C	A	Y	F	I	I	N	S	I	O	S	E	I	D	I	A	X
L	N	B	R	N	W	E	D	E	N	E	T	S	A	H	C	N	V
Y	M	C	E	Y	D	D	F	F	G	Q	L	I	S	B	P	T	Q
R	J	D	Z	N	F	S	E	S	E	S	D	C	M	A	L	L	N
R	A	R	E	V	E	R	B	E	R	A	T	E	D	L	L	Y	J
L	G	T	I	N	T	E	R	F	E	R	E	R	N	M	T	F	T
L	A	P	E	L	M	L	B	F	D	N	N	P	N	Y	V	V	T

A radiance encircling the head or body; a halo (7)
A slow, stately dance or music for such a dance (6)
A special quality that inspires allegiance and devotion (8)
A traveling poet, singer or musician (8)
An invasion of privacy (9)
Burnt up; burned a dead body to ashes (8)
Cautious (4)
Continued to stay; delayed; loitered (8)
Easy to do, use, or get to (10)
Exact correspondence of form on opposite sides of a dividing line (11)
Expect the best outcome (10)
Inclination to move or act in a particular way (8)
Intense or eager interest; passion (10)
Liable to fall or break down because of weakness (7)
Loaded; burdened (5)
Made smaller; lessened; reduced (10)

Meddle; hinder; prevent; intervene (9)
Models of the human body usually used in stores (8)
Not sharp or certain; hazily (7)
Part of a jacket folded back from the neckline (5)
Particularly; exactly (9)
Rolling, pitching or swaying suddenly (8)
Showing resentment and ill humor (5)
Soothing; mild; pleasant (5)
Subdued; restrained from excess (9)
Successfully; elated (12)
Teasing; prank; naughty or troublesome act (8)
To be reflected as light or sound waves (12)
To declare firmly and persistently (8)
To flow out; come forth; emit (7)
To have a conference or talk (6)
Tormented or worried; harassed (7)
Write or speak easily, smoothly and expressively (8)

Dicey's Song Vocabulary Word Search 2 Answer Key

Words are placed backwards, forward, diagonally, up and down. Clues listed below can help you find the words. Circle the hidden vocabulary words in the maze.

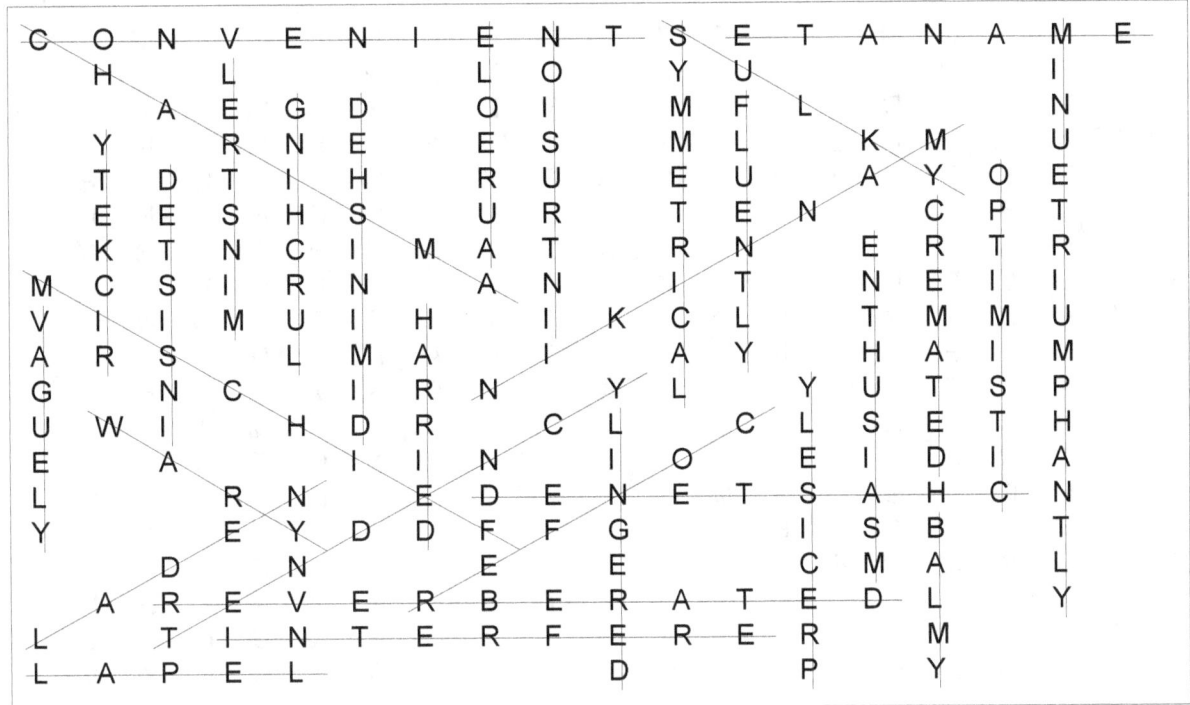

A radiance encircling the head or body; a halo (7)
A slow, stately dance or music for such a dance (6)
A special quality that inspires allegiance and devotion (8)
A traveling poet, singer or musician (8)
An invasion of privacy (9)
Burnt up; burned a dead body to ashes (8)
Cautious (4)
Continued to stay; delayed; loitered (8)
Easy to do, use, or get to (10)
Exact correspondence of form on opposite sides of a dividing line (11)
Expect the best outcome (10)
Inclination to move or act in a particular way (8)
Intense or eager interest; passion (10)
Liable to fall or break down because of weakness (7)
Loaded; burdened (5)
Made smaller; lessened; reduced (10)

Meddle; hinder; prevent; intervene (9)
Models of the human body usually used in stores (8)
Not sharp or certain; hazily (7)
Part of a jacket folded back from the neckline (5)
Particularly; exactly (9)
Rolling, pitching or swaying suddenly (8)
Showing resentment and ill humor (5)
Soothing; mild; pleasant (5)
Subdued; restrained from excess (9)
Successfully; elated (12)
Teasing; prank; naughty or troublesome act (8)
To be reflected as light or sound waves (12)
To declare firmly and persistently (8)
To flow out; come forth; emit (7)
To have a conference or talk (6)
Tormented or worried; harassed (7)
Write or speak easily, smoothly and expressively (8)

Dicey's Song Vocabulary Word Search 3

Words are placed backwards, forward, diagonally, up and down. Words listed below are included in the maze. Circle the hidden vocabulary words in the maze.

```
Y Y D M N M K C Q W L R I C K E T Y M J
H K P P H T R O N M U E M I N S T R E L
T C I D A R T N O C R V L Z S W W N A V
G S T T H G D G Y P C E D E T S I S N I
F Z R Y P L J E L S H R Y W H L V C D R
S R I B L E P A L U I B M I S C H I E F
B Y U A D C D L H L N E H J K P T R R M
H W M L D E B E R K G R Z G D L E K I F
C N P M N V I D W Y Y A W Y F F U D N Z
O H H Y E V C N H V L T L A R G N E G J
N M A C C T A A T X K E C E R W I M F L
V A N R C H R G L R S D T B D Y M A X J
E N T R I R A I U I U N T E N D E N C Y
N N L R I S N S C E I S R D N L L A O Q
I I Y E L G M E T A L G I M N W O T N R
E K D S E M R A W E L Y F O S B E E F W
N I W R L P F L U E N T L Y N N R T E X
T N E N Z S D E T A M E R C J K U N R Z
Z D I M I N I S H E D F D G S X A H W V
```

AUREOLE	HARRIED	MISCHIEF
BALMY	INSISTED	PRECISELY
CHARISMA	INTERFERE	REVERBERATED
CHASTENED	INTRUSION	RICKETY
CONFER	LADEN	SULKY
CONGEALED	LAPEL	SYMMETRICAL
CONTRADICT	LINGERED	TENDENCY
CONVENIENT	LURCHING	TRIUMPHANTLY
CREMATED	MANNIKIN	VAGUELY
DIMINISHED	MEANDERING	WARY
EMANATE	MINSTREL	
FLUENTLY	MINUET	

Dicey's Song Vocabulary Word Search 3 Answer Key

Words are placed backwards, forward, diagonally, up and down. Words listed below are included in the maze. Circle the hidden vocabulary words in the maze.

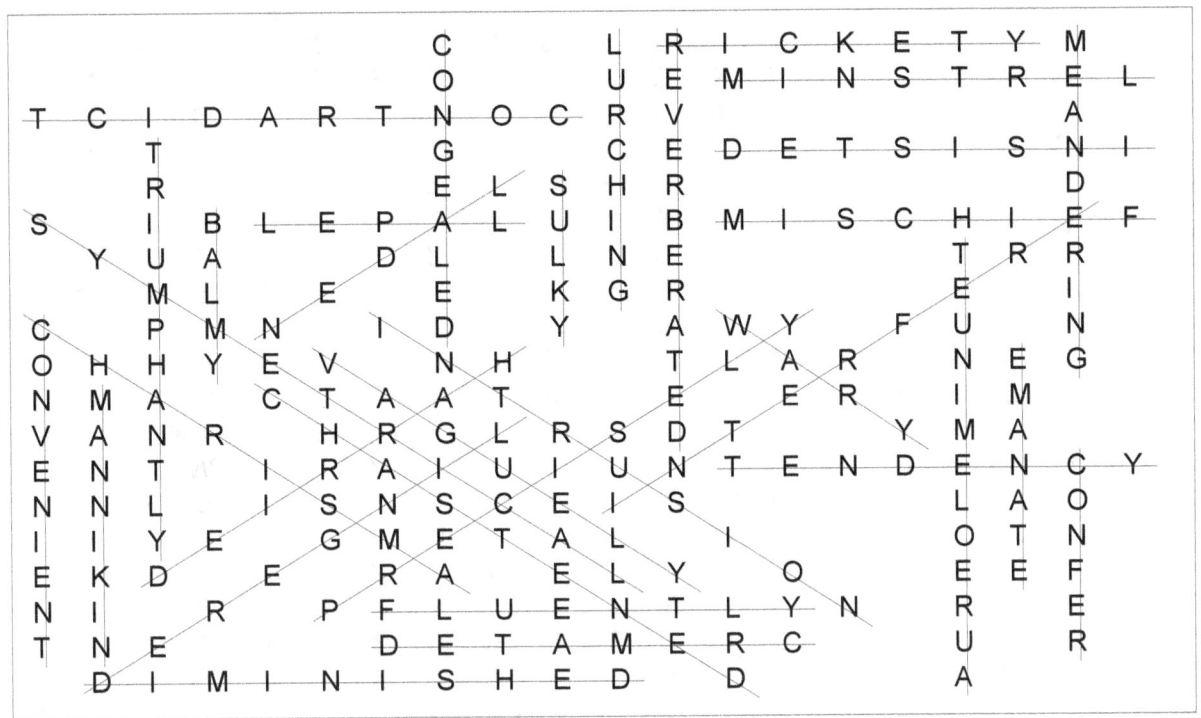

AUREOLE	HARRIED	MISCHIEF
BALMY	INSISTED	PRECISELY
CHARISMA	INTERFERE	REVERBERATED
CHASTENED	INTRUSION	RICKETY
CONFER	LADEN	SULKY
CONGEALED	LAPEL	SYMMETRICAL
CONTRADICT	LINGERED	TENDENCY
CONVENIENT	LURCHING	TRIUMPHANTLY
CREMATED	MANNIKIN	VAGUELY
DIMINISHED	MEANDERING	WARY
EMANATE	MINSTREL	
FLUENTLY	MINUET	

Dicey's Song Vocabulary Word Search 4

Words are placed backwards, forward, diagonally, up and down. Words listed below are included in the maze. Circle the hidden vocabulary words in the maze.

```
D E C E I T F U L N E S S W D Q C X V Z
R Y H Y D X F U K G A J C D E G H T A M
E I X R W J R L J X K U L O D B A C G P
V D C D M C P A U R M W R V N Y S I U V
E K N K H L I N G E R E D E U F T D E Y
R B I I E K C T Y T N Z G D O V E A L T
B Y N Q X T D I L C K T L Z F L N R Y W
E G T M C L Y C E L H X L C B V E T T P
R C R C I K M I S A Q A F Y M V D N C X
A D U S M N I P I C X S R L U P E O I S
T Y S E N D S A C I F K I I D D I C T C
E M I M C Q C T E R Y N K K S Z R K S T
D L O A W T H I R T T Q L S Y M R W I K
M A N N I K I N P E N T H U S I A S M G
J B L A T J E G R M L E K L N R H Z I F
K V A T B D F F K M G U V K Y Y K X T Y
H Q P E A H E G W Y L N C Y P L V Z P H
Q H E L M R W Z K S T I B R Z F K F O L
Z Q L D E T S I S N I M T E N D E N C Y
```

ANTICIPATING	FLUENTLY	MINUET
AUREOLE	HARRIED	MISCHIEF
BALMY	INSISTED	OPTIMISTIC
CHARISMA	INTERFERE	PRECISELY
CHASTENED	INTRUSION	REVERBERATED
CONFER	LADEN	RICKETY
CONTRADICT	LAPEL	SULKY
DECEITFULNESS	LINGERED	SYMMETRICAL
DUMBFOUNDED	LURCHING	TENDENCY
EMANATE	MANNIKIN	VAGUELY
ENTHUSIASM	MINSTREL	WARY

Dicey's Song Vocabulary Word Search 4 Answer Key

Words are placed backwards, forward, diagonally, up and down. Words listed below are included in the maze. Circle the hidden vocabulary words in the maze.

ANTICIPATING	FLUENTLY	MINUET
AUREOLE	HARRIED	MISCHIEF
BALMY	INSISTED	OPTIMISTIC
CHARISMA	INTERFERE	PRECISELY
CHASTENED	INTRUSION	REVERBERATED
CONFER	LADEN	RICKETY
CONTRADICT	LAPEL	SULKY
DECEITFULNESS	LINGERED	SYMMETRICAL
DUMBFOUNDED	LURCHING	TENDENCY
EMANATE	MANNIKIN	VAGUELY
ENTHUSIASM	MINSTREL	WARY

Dicey's Song Vocabulary Crossword 1

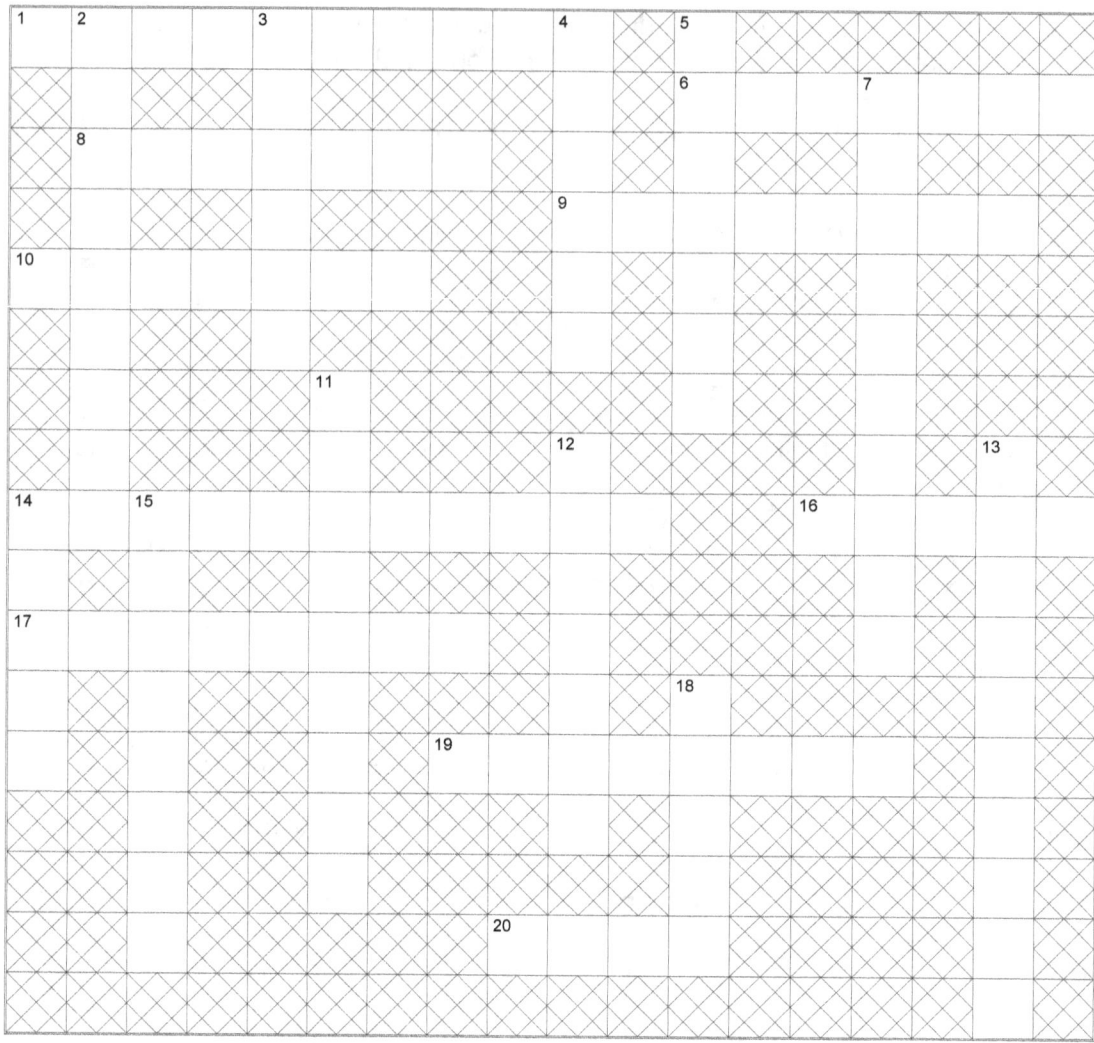

Across
1. Expect the best outcome
6. A radiance encircling the head or body; a halo
8. To flow out; come forth; emit
9. Write or speak easily, smoothly and expressively
10. Liable to fall or break down because of weakness
14. Exact correspondence of form on opposite sides of a dividing line
16. Loaded; burdened
17. Continued to stay; delayed; loitered
19. Burnt up; burned a dead body to ashes
20. Cautious

Down
2. Particularly; exactly
3. A slow, stately dance or music for such a dance
4. To have a conference or talk
5. Not sharp or certain; hazily
7. Intense or eager interest; passion
11. Meddle; hinder; prevent; intervene
12. Tormented or worried; harassed
13. An aimless wandering; rambling
14. Showing resentment and ill humor
15. Models of the human body usually used in stores
18. Soothing; mild; pleasant

Dicey's Song Vocabulary Crossword 1 Answer Key

	1 O	2 P	T	3 I	M	I	S	T	4 I	C	5 V				
		R		I					O		6 A	U	R	7 E	O	L	E
		8 E	M	A	N	A	T	E	N		G			N	
		C		U					9 F	L	U	E	N	T	L	Y
	10 R	I	C	K	E	T	Y		E		E			H	
		S		T					R		L			U	
		E			11 I						Y			S		13 M
		L			N			12 H					I		16 L	A	D	E	N
14 S	Y	15 M	M	E	T	R	I	C	A	L			
U		A		E				R			S		A	
17 L	I	N	G	E	R	E	D	R		18 B	M		N	
K		N		F				I		B			D	
Y		I		E		19 C	R	E	M	A	T	E	D		E
		K		R				D		L				R
		I		E						M				I
						20 W	A	R	Y					N
		N												G

Across
1. Expect the best outcome
6. A radiance encircling the head or body; a halo
8. To flow out; come forth; emit
9. Write or speak easily, smoothly and expressively
10. Liable to fall or break down because of weakness
14. Exact correspondence of form on opposite sides of a dividing line
16. Loaded; burdened
17. Continued to stay; delayed; loitered
19. Burnt up; burned a dead body to ashes
20. Cautious

Down
2. Particularly; exactly
3. A slow, stately dance or music for such a dance
4. To have a conference or talk
5. Not sharp or certain; hazily
7. Intense or eager interest; passion
11. Meddle; hinder; prevent; intervene
12. Tormented or worried; harassed
13. An aimless wandering; rambling
14. Showing resentment and ill humor
15. Models of the human body usually used in stores
18. Soothing; mild; pleasant

Dicey's Song Vocabulary Crossword 2

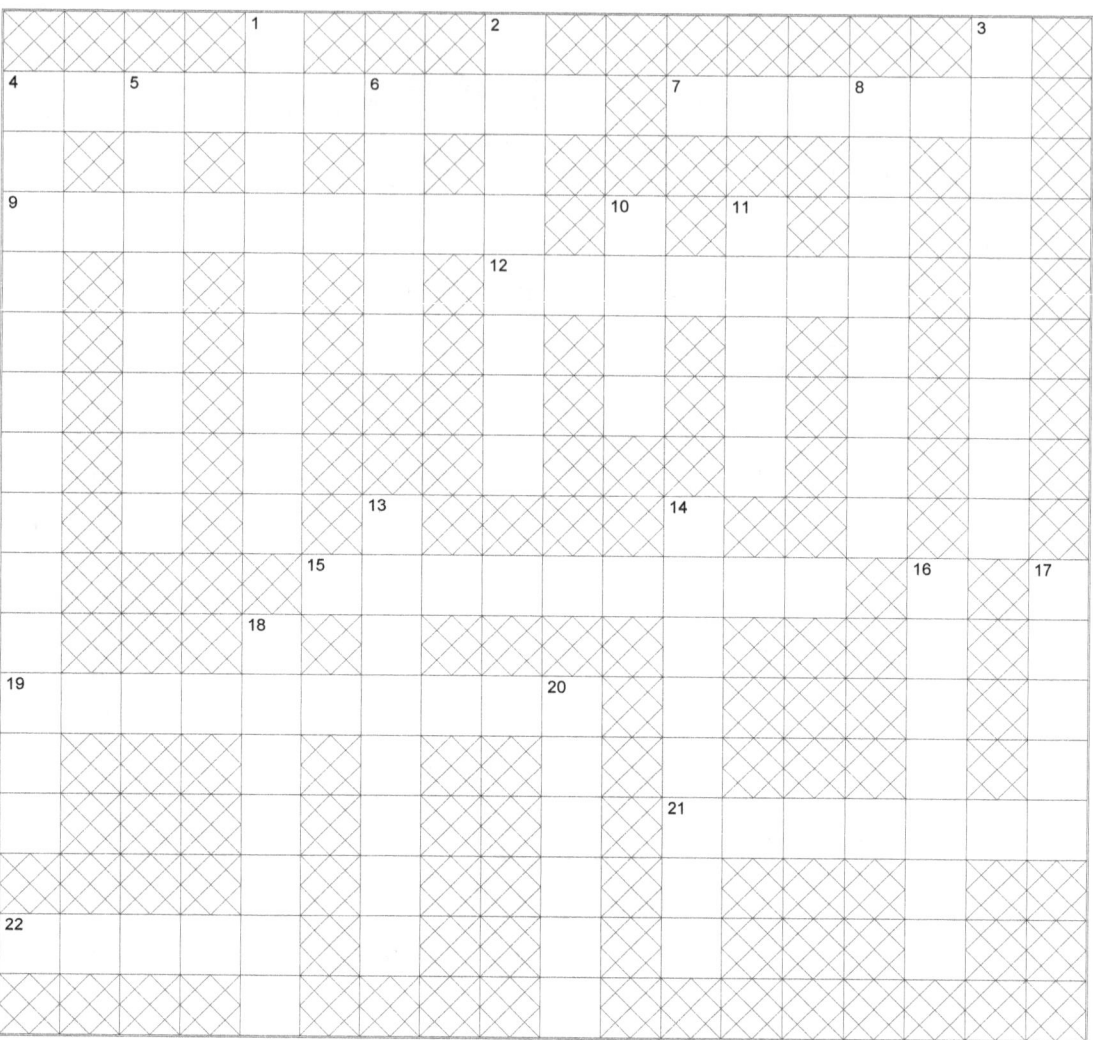

Across
4. Made smaller; lessened; reduced
7. To have a conference or talk
9. Coagulated; solidified or thickened
12. To flow out; come forth; emit
15. An invasion of privacy
19. Intense or eager interest; passion
21. Liable to fall or break down because of weakness
22. Part of a jacket folded back from the neckline

Down
1. Meddle; hinder; prevent; intervene
2. Inclination to move or act in a particular way
3. Particularly; exactly
4. Dishonest action or trick; fraud or lie
5. Models of the human body usually used in stores
6. Showing resentment and ill humor
8. Write or speak easily, smoothly and expressively
10. Cautious
11. Loaded; burdened
13. To declare firmly and persistently
14. Continued to stay; delayed; loitered
16. Not sharp or certain; hazily
17. Soothing; mild; pleasant
18. A radiance encircling the head or body; a halo
20. A slow, stately dance or music for such a dance

Dicey's Song Vocabulary Crossword 2 Answer Key

		1 I		2 T				3 P
4 D	5 I M	I	N	6 I S	H	E D	7 C O N	8 F E R
E	A	T		U		N		L		E
9 C	O N	G	E	A	L	E D	10 W	11 L	U	C
E	N	R		K		12 E	M A N	A T	E	I
I	I	F		Y		N	R	D	N	S
T	K	E				C	Y	E	T	E
F	I	R				Y		N	L	L
U	N	E		13 I			14 L		Y	Y
L			15 I N	T R U S	I O N				16 V	17 B
N		18 A	S			N			A	A
19 E	N T	H U S	I A S	M		G			G	L
S		R	S			I			E	U	M
S		E	T			N		21 R I C	K	E T Y
		O	E			U		E		L
22 L	A P E	L		D		E		D		Y
		E				T				

Across

4. Made smaller; lessened; reduced
7. To have a conference or talk
9. Coagulated; solidified or thickened
12. To flow out; come forth; emit
15. An invasion of privacy
19. Intense or eager interest; passion
21. Liable to fall or break down because of weakness
22. Part of a jacket folded back from the neckline

Down

1. Meddle; hinder; prevent; intervene
2. Inclination to move or act in a particular way
3. Particularly; exactly
4. Dishonest action or trick; fraud or lie
5. Models of the human body usually used in stores
6. Showing resentment and ill humor
8. Write or speak easily, smoothly and expressively
10. Cautious
11. Loaded; burdened
13. To declare firmly and persistently
14. Continued to stay; delayed; loitered
16. Not sharp or certain; hazily
17. Soothing; mild; pleasant
18. A radiance encircling the head or body; a halo
20. A slow, stately dance or music for such a dance

Dicey's Song Vocabulary Crossword 3

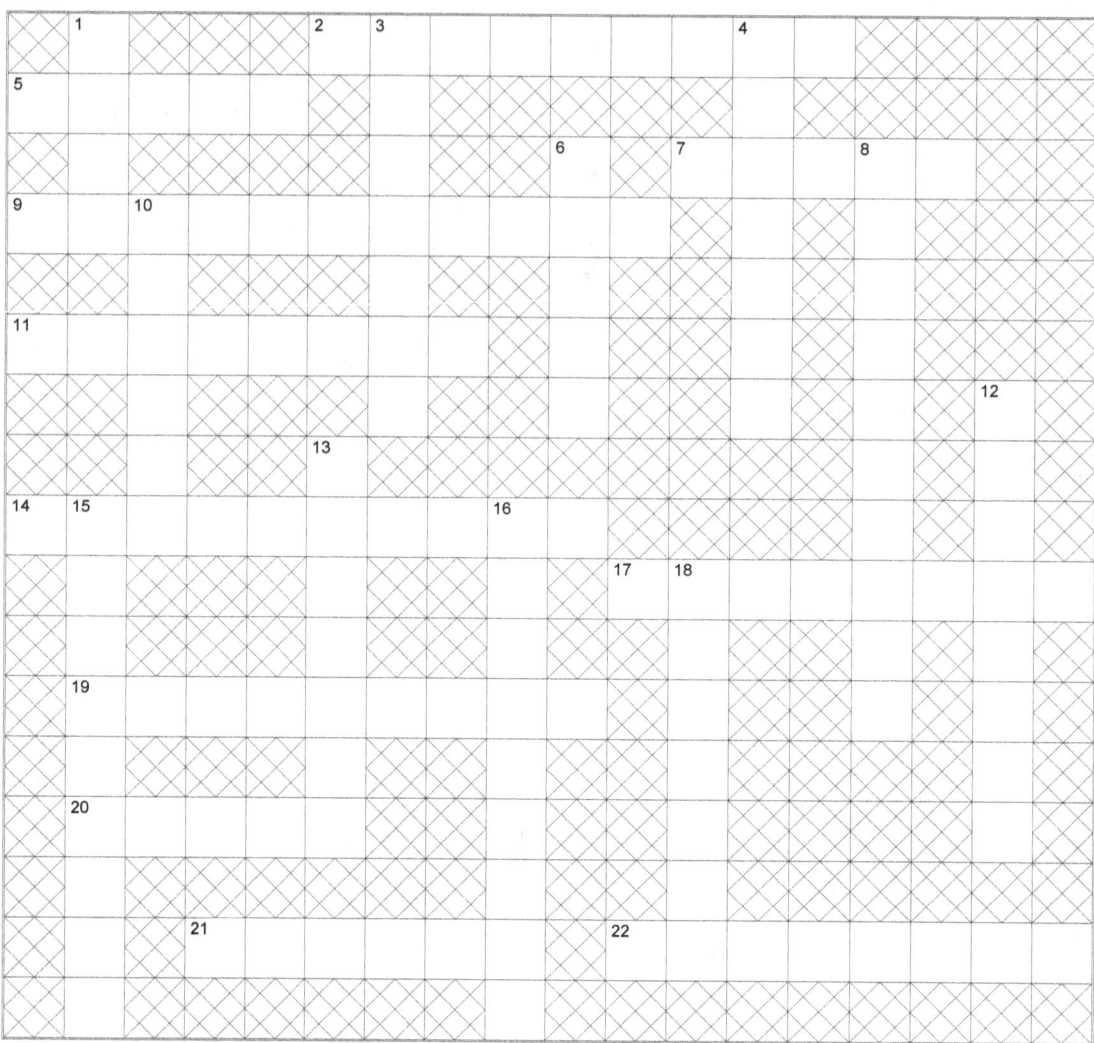

Across
2. Subdued; restrained from excess
5. Loaded; burdened
7. Soothing; mild; pleasant
9. Exact correspondence of form on opposite sides of a dividing line
11. Continued to stay; delayed; loitered
14. Expect the best outcome
17. Models of the human body usually used in stores
19. Coagulated; solidified or thickened
20. Showing resentment and ill humor
21. To have a conference or talk
22. Inclination to move or act in a particular way

Down
1. Cautious
3. Tormented or worried; harassed
4. To flow out; come forth; emit
6. Part of a jacket folded back from the neckline
8. An aimless wandering; rambling
10. A slow, stately dance or music for such a dance
12. To declare firmly and persistently
13. Liable to fall or break down because of weakness
15. Particularly; exactly
16. Meddle; hinder; prevent; intervene
18. A radiance encircling the head or body; a halo

Dicey's Song Vocabulary Crossword 3 Answer Key

	1 W		2 C	3 H	A	S	T	E	4 N	E	D			
5 L	A	D	E	N		A				E	M			
	R			R				6 L		7 B	A	L	8 M	Y
9 S	Y	10 M	M	E	T	R	I	C	A	L		N		E
		I				I		P		A		A		
11 L	I	N	G	E	R	E	D		E		T		N	
		U				D		L		E		D		12 I
		E			13 R						E		N	
14 O	15 P	T	I	M	I	S	T	16 I	C			R		S
	R				C			N		17 M	18 A	N	N	I	K	I	N
	E				K			T		U		N		S
	19 C	O	N	G	E	A	L	E	D	R		G		T
	I				T			R		E				E
	20 S	U	L	K	Y			F		O				D
	E							E		L				
	L		21 C	O	N	F	E	R		22 T	E	N	D	E	N	C	Y
	Y							E						

Across
2. Subdued; restrained from excess
5. Loaded; burdened
7. Soothing; mild; pleasant
9. Exact correspondence of form on opposite sides of a dividing line
11. Continued to stay; delayed; loitered
14. Expect the best outcome
17. Models of the human body usually used in stores
19. Coagulated; solidified or thickened
20. Showing resentment and ill humor
21. To have a conference or talk
22. Inclination to move or act in a particular way

Down
1. Cautious
3. Tormented or worried; harassed
4. To flow out; come forth; emit
6. Part of a jacket folded back from the neckline
8. An aimless wandering; rambling
10. A slow, stately dance or music for such a dance
12. To declare firmly and persistently
13. Liable to fall or break down because of weakness
15. Particularly; exactly
16. Meddle; hinder; prevent; intervene
18. A radiance encircling the head or body; a halo

Dicey's Song Vocabulary Crossword 4

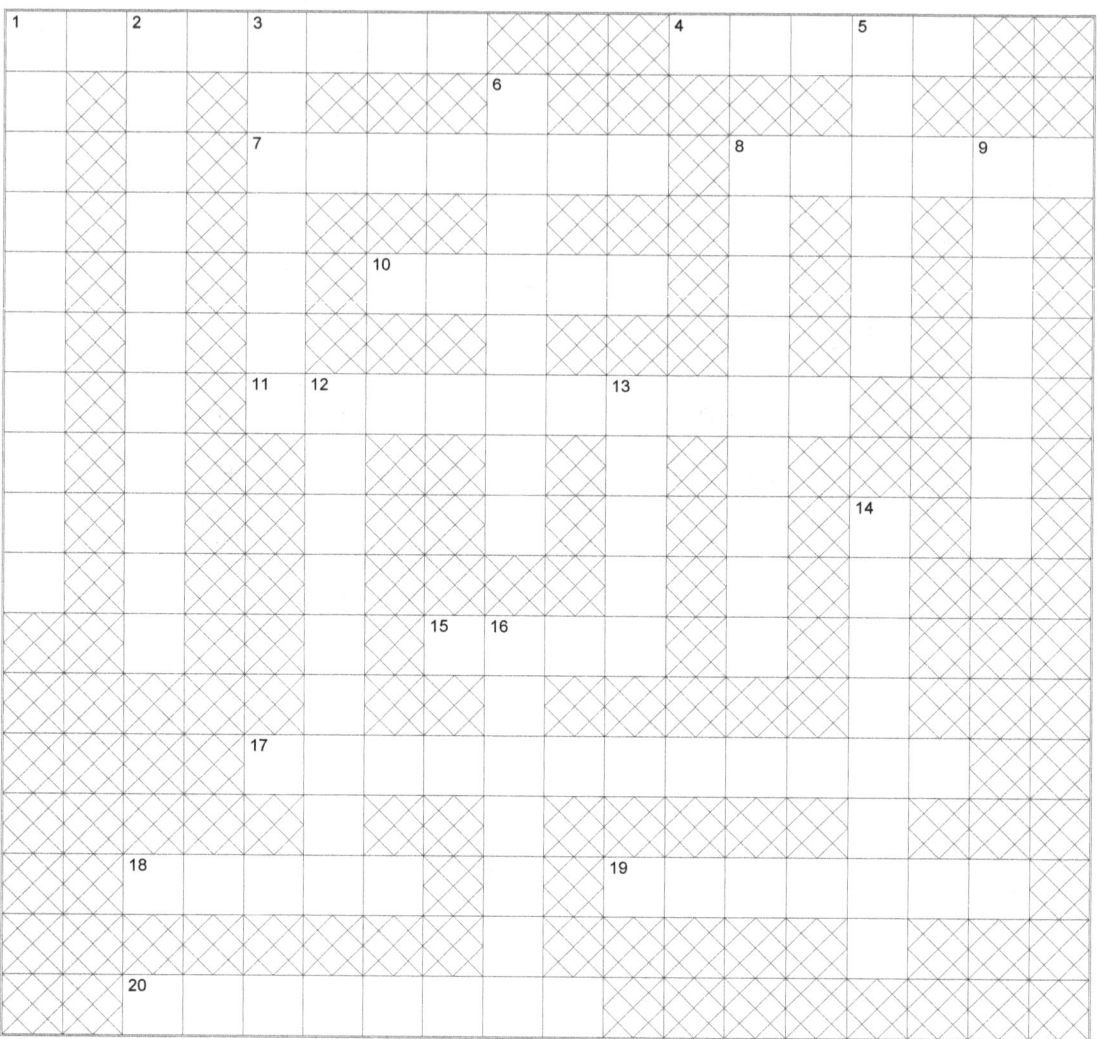

Across
1. Teasing; prank; naughty or troublesome act
4. Soothing; mild; pleasant
7. Liable to fall or break down because of weakness
8. To have a conference or talk
10. Loaded; burdened
11. Made smaller; lessened; reduced
15. Cautious
17. To be reflected as light or sound waves
18. Part of a jacket folded back from the neckline
19. Not sharp or certain; hazily
20. A traveling poet, singer or musician

Down
1. An aimless wandering; rambling
2. Exact correspondence of form on opposite sides of a dividing line
3. Tormented or worried; harassed
5. A slow, stately dance or music for such a dance
6. Inclination to move or act in a particular way
8. Coagulated; solidified or thickened
9. To flow out; come forth; emit
12. Meddle; hinder; prevent; intervene
13. Showing resentment and ill humor
14. Continued to stay; delayed; loitered
16. A radiance encircling the head or body; a halo

Dicey's Song Vocabulary Crossword 4 Answer Key

Across
1. Teasing; prank; naughty or troublesome act
4. Soothing; mild; pleasant
7. Liable to fall or break down because of weakness
8. To have a conference or talk
10. Loaded; burdened
11. Made smaller; lessened; reduced
15. Cautious
17. To be reflected as light or sound waves
18. Part of a jacket folded back from the neckline
19. Not sharp or certain; hazily
20. A traveling poet, singer or musician

Down
1. An aimless wandering; rambling
2. Exact correspondence of form on opposite sides of a dividing line
3. Tormented or worried; harassed
5. A slow, stately dance or music for such a dance
6. Inclination to move or act in a particular way
8. Coagulated; solidified or thickened
9. To flow out; come forth; emit
12. Meddle; hinder; prevent; intervene
13. Showing resentment and ill humor
14. Continued to stay; delayed; loitered
16. A radiance encircling the head or body; a halo

Dicey's Song Vocabulary Juggle Letters 1

1. EOLERAU = 1. _____
   A radiance encircling the head or body; a halo

2. RIRDHAE = 2. _____
   Tormented or worried; harassed

3. DNGOAEECL = 3. _____
   Coagulated; solidified or thickened

4. APLEL = 4. _____
   Part of a jacket folded back from the neckline

5. NEALD = 5. _____
   Loaded; burdened

6. MBYAL = 6. _____
   Soothing; mild; pleasant

7. HANESCETD = 7. _____
   Subdued; restrained from excess

8. ENTENVICON = 8. _____
   Easy to do, use, or get to

9. RREEVBEDARET = 9. _____
   To be reflected as light or sound waves

10. IRPESELCY = 10. _____
    Particularly; exactly

11. INNNAKMI = 11. _____
    Models of the human body usually used in stores

12. AATGCIIPNNTI = 12. _____
    Looking forward to or expecting

13. BEDDFUMDOUN = 13. _____
    Made speechless by shocking; amazed

14. CTKYEIR = 14. _____
    Liable to fall or break down because of weakness

15. MDCETEAR = 15. _____
    Burnt up; burned a dead body to ashes

Dicey's Song Vocabulary Juggle Letters 1 Answer Key

1. EOLERAU = 1. AUREOLE
A radiance encircling the head or body; a halo

2. RIRDHAE = 2. HARRIED
Tormented or worried; harassed

3. DNGOAEECL = 3. CONGEALED
Coagulated; solidified or thickened

4. APLEL = 4. LAPEL
Part of a jacket folded back from the neckline

5. NEALD = 5. LADEN
Loaded; burdened

6. MBYAL = 6. BALMY
Soothing; mild; pleasant

7. HANESCETD = 7. CHASTENED
Subdued; restrained from excess

8. ENTENVICON = 8. CONVENIENT
Easy to do, use, or get to

9. RREEVBEDARET = 9. REVERBERATED
To be reflected as light or sound waves

10. IRPESELCY = 10. PRECISELY
Particularly; exactly

11. INNNAKMI = 11. MANNIKIN
Models of the human body usually used in stores

12. AATGCIIPNNTI = 12. ANTICIPATING
Looking forward to or expecting

13. BEDDFUMDOUN = 13. DUMBFOUNDED
Made speechless by shocking; amazed

14. CTKYEIR = 14. RICKETY
Liable to fall or break down because of weakness

15. MDCETEAR = 15. CREMATED
Burnt up; burned a dead body to ashes

Dicey's Song Vocabulary Juggle Letters 2

1. ODINATCCTR = 1. _____
   Oppose verbally; go against; assert the opposite

2. YULKS = 2. _____
   Showing resentment and ill humor

3. RCYIMAMSTEL = 3. _____
   Exact correspondence of form on opposite sides of a dividing line

4. ATNAMEE = 4. _____
   To flow out; come forth; emit

5. IHDNEMIDSI = 5. _____
   Made smaller; lessened; reduced

6. SASHUTENMI = 6. _____
   Intense or eager interest; passion

7. IMPTHTLNRAUY = 7. _____
   Successfully; elated

8. NATGNTCPIIIA = 8. _____
   Looking forward to or expecting

9. ORFCNE = 9. _____
   To have a conference or talk

10. NEEDCUEIFSLTS =10. _____
    Dishonest action or trick; fraud or lie

11. DENLGEIR =11. _____
    Continued to stay; delayed; loitered

12. LRPISCEEY =12. _____
    Particularly; exactly

13. EEENFRRIT =13. _____
    Meddle; hinder; prevent; intervene

14. NTLSREIM =14. _____
    A traveling poet, singer or musician

15. IEAHDRR =15. _____
    Tormented or worried; harassed

Dicey's Song Vocabulary Juggle Letters 2 Answer Key

1. ODINATCCTR = 1. CONTRADICT
   Oppose verbally; go against; assert the opposite

2. YULKS = 2. SULKY
   Showing resentment and ill humor

3. RCYIMAMSTEL = 3. SYMMETRICAL
   Exact correspondence of form on opposite sides of a dividing line

4. ATNAMEE = 4. EMANATE
   To flow out; come forth; emit

5. IHDNEMIDSI = 5. DIMINISHED
   Made smaller; lessened; reduced

6. SASHUTENMI = 6. ENTHUSIASM
   Intense or eager interest; passion

7. IMPTHTLNRAUY = 7. TRIUMPHANTLY
   Successfully; elated

8. NATGNTCPIIIA = 8. ANTICIPATING
   Looking forward to or expecting

9. ORFCNE = 9. CONFER
   To have a conference or talk

10. NEEDCUEIFSLTS = 10. DECEITFULNESS
    Dishonest action or trick; fraud or lie

11. DENLGEIR = 11. LINGERED
    Continued to stay; delayed; loitered

12. LRPISCEEY = 12. PRECISELY
    Particularly; exactly

13. EEENFRRIT = 13. INTERFERE
    Meddle; hinder; prevent; intervene

14. NTLSREIM = 14. MINSTREL
    A traveling poet, singer or musician

15. IEAHDRR = 15. HARRIED
    Tormented or worried; harassed

Dicey's Song Vocabulary Juggle Letters 3

1. DIARENEGMN = 1. _____
   An aimless wandering; rambling

2. TIDARTCNOC = 2. _____
   Oppose verbally; go against; assert the opposite

3. OECFRN = 3. _____
   To have a conference or talk

4. NTELYLFU = 4. _____
   Write or speak easily, smoothly and expressively

5. SEUHNSTIMA = 5. _____
   Intense or eager interest; passion

6. SIISEDTN = 6. _____
   To declare firmly and persistently

7. EMDDIIINSH = 7. _____
   Made smaller; lessened; reduced

8. IFUSCELTESEDN = 8. _____
   Dishonest action or trick; fraud or lie

9. ERAIRDH = 9. _____
   Tormented or worried; harassed

10. NDECYTEN = 10. _____
    Inclination to move or act in a particular way

11. EETRREFNI = 11. _____
    Meddle; hinder; prevent; intervene

12. EDRGELNI = 12. _____
    Continued to stay; delayed; loitered

13. SIOMICTPTI = 13. _____
    Expect the best outcome

14. INUMET = 14. _____
    A slow, stately dance or music for such a dance

15. VENTECIONN = 15. _____
    Easy to do, use, or get to

Dicey's Song Vocabulary Juggle Letters 3 Answer Key

1. DIARENEGMN = 1. MEANDERING
   An aimless wandering; rambling

2. TIDARTCNOC = 2. CONTRADICT
   Oppose verbally; go against; assert the opposite

3. OECFRN = 3. CONFER
   To have a conference or talk

4. NTELYLFU = 4. FLUENTLY
   Write or speak easily, smoothly and expressively

5. SEUHNSTIMA = 5. ENTHUSIASM
   Intense or eager interest; passion

6. SIISEDTN = 6. INSISTED
   To declare firmly and persistently

7. EMDDIIINSH = 7. DIMINISHED
   Made smaller; lessened; reduced

8. IFUSCELTESEDN = 8. DECEITFULNESS
   Dishonest action or trick; fraud or lie

9. ERAIRDH = 9. HARRIED
   Tormented or worried; harassed

10. NDECYTEN = 10. TENDENCY
    Inclination to move or act in a particular way

11. EETRREFNI = 11. INTERFERE
    Meddle; hinder; prevent; intervene

12. EDRGELNI = 12. LINGERED
    Continued to stay; delayed; loitered

13. SIOMICTPTI = 13. OPTIMISTIC
    Expect the best outcome

14. INUMET = 14. MINUET
    A slow, stately dance or music for such a dance

15. VENTECIONN = 15. CONVENIENT
    Easy to do, use, or get to

Dicey's Song Vocabulary Juggle Letters 4

1. IEENLDRG = 1. _____
   Continued to stay; delayed; loitered

2. NOUDDDBEMUF = 2. _____
   Made speechless by shocking; amazed

3. IMTPSIOTIC = 3. _____
   Expect the best outcome

4. ANDLE = 4. _____
   Loaded; burdened

5. ETAMREDC = 5. _____
   Burnt up; burned a dead body to ashes

6. IMYLUTTPNHRA = 6. _____
   Successfully; elated

7. YRWA = 7. _____
   Cautious

8. HSDECNTEA = 8. _____
   Subdued; restrained from excess

9. NNINMKAI = 9. _____
   Models of the human body usually used in stores

10. IIUSNONTR = 10. _____
    An invasion of privacy

11. LMBYA = 11. _____
    Soothing; mild; pleasant

12. RSNLITEM = 12. _____
    A traveling poet, singer or musician

13. EDTRREVRBEAE = 13. _____
    To be reflected as light or sound waves

14. DEENNYCT = 14. _____
    Inclination to move or act in a particular way

15. REELUAO = 15. _____
    A radiance encircling the head or body; a halo

Dicey's Song Vocabulary Juggle Letters 4 Answer Key

1. IEENLDRG = 1. LINGERED
   Continued to stay; delayed; loitered

2. NOUDDDBEMUF = 2. DUMBFOUNDED
   Made speechless by shocking; amazed

3. IMTPSIOTIC = 3. OPTIMISTIC
   Expect the best outcome

4. ANDLE = 4. LADEN
   Loaded; burdened

5. ETAMREDC = 5. CREMATED
   Burnt up; burned a dead body to ashes

6. IMYLUTTPNHRA = 6. TRIUMPHANTLY
   Successfully; elated

7. YRWA = 7. WARY
   Cautious

8. HSDECNTEA = 8. CHASTENED
   Subdued; restrained from excess

9. NNINMKAI = 9. MANNIKIN
   Models of the human body usually used in stores

10. IIUSNONTR = 10. INTRUSION
    An invasion of privacy

11. LMBYA = 11. BALMY
    Soothing; mild; pleasant

12. RSNLITEM = 12. MINSTREL
    A traveling poet, singer or musician

13. EDTRREVRBEAE = 13. REVERBERATED
    To be reflected as light or sound waves

14. DEENNYCT = 14. TENDENCY
    Inclination to move or act in a particular way

15. REELUAO = 15. AUREOLE
    A radiance encircling the head or body; a halo

ANTICIPATING	Looking forward to or expecting
AUREOLE	A radiance encircling the head or body; a halo
BALMY	Soothing; mild; pleasant
CHARISMA	A special quality that inspires allegiance and devotion
CHASTENED	Subdued; restrained from excess
CONFER	To have a conference or talk

CONGEALED	Coagulated; solidified or thickened
CONTRADICT	Oppose verbally; go against; assert the opposite
CONVENIENT	Easy to do, use, or get to
CREMATED	Burnt up; burned a dead body to ashes
DECEITFULNESS	Dishonest action or trick; fraud or lie
DIMINISHED	Made smaller; lessened; reduced

DUMBFOUNDED	Made speechless by shocking; amazed
EMANATE	To flow out; come forth; emit
ENTHUSIASM	Intense or eager interest; passion
FLUENTLY	Write or speak easily, smoothly and expressively
HARRIED	Tormented or worried; harassed
INSISTED	To declare firmly and persistently

INTERFERE	Meddle; hinder; prevent; intervene
INTRUSION	An invasion of privacy
LADEN	Loaded; burdened
LAPEL	Part of a jacket folded back from the neckline
LINGERED	Continued to stay; delayed; loitered
LURCHING	Rolling, pitching or swaying suddenly

MANNIKIN	Models of the human body usually used in stores
MEANDERING	An aimless wandering; rambling
MINSTREL	A traveling poet, singer or musician
MINUET	A slow, stately dance or music for such a dance
MISCHIEF	Teasing; prank; naughty or troublesome act
OPTIMISTIC	Expect the best outcome

PRECISELY	Particularly; exactly
REVERBERATED	To be reflected as light or sound waves
RICKETY	Liable to fall or break down because of weakness
SULKY	Showing resentment and ill humor
SYMMETRICAL	Exact correspondence of form on opposite sides of a dividing line
TENDENCY	Inclination to move or act in a particular way

TRIUMPHANTLY	Successfully; elated
VAGUELY	Not sharp or certain; hazily
WARY	Cautious

Dicey's Song Vocabulary

DUMBFOUNDED	CONGEALED	DECEITFULNESS	ANTICIPATING	VAGUELY
CONFER	RICKETY	LURCHING	AUREOLE	MISCHIEF
MINUET	REVERBERATED	FREE SPACE	PRECISELY	ENTHUSIASM
MINSTREL	WARY	MANNIKIN	TENDENCY	CONVENIENT
EMANATE	BALMY	INTERFERE	MEANDERING	LINGERED

Dicey's Song Vocabulary

INTRUSION	LAPEL	OPTIMISTIC	HARRIED	CHARISMA
DIMINISHED	LADEN	TRIUMPHANTLY	SULKY	FLUENTLY
CREMATED	CHASTENED	FREE SPACE	CONTRADICT	LINGERED
MEANDERING	INTERFERE	BALMY	EMANATE	CONVENIENT
TENDENCY	MANNIKIN	WARY	MINSTREL	ENTHUSIASM

Dicey's Song Vocabulary

INTRUSION	LURCHING	INSISTED	PRECISELY	MANNIKIN
CONVENIENT	DUMBFOUNDED	FLUENTLY	WARY	DIMINISHED
MEANDERING	CREMATED	FREE SPACE	CHARISMA	SYMMETRICAL
LADEN	CONFER	AUREOLE	LAPEL	EMANATE
REVERBERATED	CHASTENED	OPTIMISTIC	VAGUELY	RICKETY

Dicey's Song Vocabulary

CONTRADICT	BALMY	MISCHIEF	DECEITFULNESS	INTERFERE
MINSTREL	MINUET	TENDENCY	SULKY	LINGERED
ANTICIPATING	CONGEALED	FREE SPACE	HARRIED	RICKETY
VAGUELY	OPTIMISTIC	CHASTENED	REVERBERATED	EMANATE
LAPEL	AUREOLE	CONFER	LADEN	SYMMETRICAL

Dicey's Song Vocabulary

DECEITFULNESS	INTRUSION	CHARISMA	RICKETY	LADEN
VAGUELY	FLUENTLY	CONVENIENT	CONGEALED	SYMMETRICAL
ANTICIPATING	TRIUMPHANTLY	FREE SPACE	EMANATE	TENDENCY
CHASTENED	LAPEL	DUMBFOUNDED	CONFER	HARRIED
INTERFERE	MINUET	MINSTREL	REVERBERATED	CONTRADICT

Dicey's Song Vocabulary

AUREOLE	DIMINISHED	ENTHUSIASM	PRECISELY	CREMATED
SULKY	LURCHING	MEANDERING	OPTIMISTIC	LINGERED
INSISTED	MANNIKIN	FREE SPACE	WARY	CONTRADICT
REVERBERATED	MINSTREL	MINUET	INTERFERE	HARRIED
CONFER	DUMBFOUNDED	LAPEL	CHASTENED	TENDENCY

Dicey's Song Vocabulary

CONVENIENT	INTRUSION	PRECISELY	MISCHIEF	FLUENTLY
ANTICIPATING	SYMMETRICAL	DIMINISHED	CREMATED	REVERBERATED
MINSTREL	TRIUMPHANTLY	FREE SPACE	LADEN	CHASTENED
EMANATE	DECEITFULNESS	MEANDERING	DUMBFOUNDED	OPTIMISTIC
LURCHING	BALMY	VAGUELY	HARRIED	MANNIKIN

Dicey's Song Vocabulary

RICKETY	CONTRADICT	LINGERED	ENTHUSIASM	MINUET
CONFER	LAPEL	WARY	AUREOLE	CHARISMA
CONGEALED	SULKY	FREE SPACE	INTERFERE	MANNIKIN
HARRIED	VAGUELY	BALMY	LURCHING	OPTIMISTIC
DUMBFOUNDED	MEANDERING	DECEITFULNESS	EMANATE	CHASTENED

Dicey's Song Vocabulary

BALMY	SYMMETRICAL	AUREOLE	ANTICIPATING	WARY
OPTIMISTIC	LINGERED	CONGEALED	TRIUMPHANTLY	MANNIKIN
CHARISMA	TENDENCY	FREE SPACE	DECEITFULNESS	MINSTREL
CHASTENED	MINUET	LURCHING	CONFER	REVERBERATED
LADEN	VAGUELY	INSISTED	FLUENTLY	MEANDERING

Dicey's Song Vocabulary

INTRUSION	CREMATED	CONTRADICT	DIMINISHED	HARRIED
DUMBFOUNDED	PRECISELY	MISCHIEF	INTERFERE	RICKETY
CONVENIENT	ENTHUSIASM	FREE SPACE	SULKY	MEANDERING
FLUENTLY	INSISTED	VAGUELY	LADEN	REVERBERATED
CONFER	LURCHING	MINUET	CHASTENED	MINSTREL

Dicey's Song Vocabulary

MINSTREL	OPTIMISTIC	TENDENCY	EMANATE	LAPEL
SYMMETRICAL	SULKY	PRECISELY	LURCHING	INTRUSION
HARRIED	DUMBFOUNDED	FREE SPACE	RICKETY	WARY
CONGEALED	MANNIKIN	MINUET	CONVENIENT	LADEN
LINGERED	CHARISMA	VAGUELY	FLUENTLY	ANTICIPATING

Dicey's Song Vocabulary

CHASTENED	BALMY	CONFER	TRIUMPHANTLY	ENTHUSIASM
INTERFERE	CREMATED	DECEITFULNESS	REVERBERATED	INSISTED
MEANDERING	DIMINISHED	FREE SPACE	CONTRADICT	ANTICIPATING
FLUENTLY	VAGUELY	CHARISMA	LINGERED	LADEN
CONVENIENT	MINUET	MANNIKIN	CONGEALED	WARY

Copyrighted

Dicey's Song Vocabulary

INSISTED	INTERFERE	INTRUSION	MEANDERING	AUREOLE
CONTRADICT	CONGEALED	RICKETY	CHASTENED	BALMY
VAGUELY	LAPEL	FREE SPACE	CONVENIENT	CREMATED
TENDENCY	MANNIKIN	TRIUMPHANTLY	MISCHIEF	MINSTREL
DUMBFOUNDED	SULKY	DECEITFULNESS	EMANATE	LURCHING

Dicey's Song Vocabulary

REVERBERATED	ANTICIPATING	HARRIED	FLUENTLY	LADEN
CHARISMA	DIMINISHED	ENTHUSIASM	OPTIMISTIC	CONFER
LINGERED	PRECISELY	FREE SPACE	MINUET	LURCHING
EMANATE	DECEITFULNESS	SULKY	DUMBFOUNDED	MINSTREL
MISCHIEF	TRIUMPHANTLY	MANNIKIN	TENDENCY	CREMATED

Dicey's Song Vocabulary

MINUET	LADEN	CREMATED	OPTIMISTIC	TRIUMPHANTLY
CONGEALED	DUMBFOUNDED	INSISTED	LINGERED	SYMMETRICAL
CHASTENED	MISCHIEF	FREE SPACE	ANTICIPATING	CONTRADICT
LAPEL	WARY	AUREOLE	EMANATE	INTRUSION
TENDENCY	MEANDERING	PRECISELY	REVERBERATED	LURCHING

Dicey's Song Vocabulary

ENTHUSIASM	CHARISMA	CONVENIENT	INTERFERE	DECEITFULNESS
MANNIKIN	MINSTREL	DIMINISHED	SULKY	RICKETY
VAGUELY	FLUENTLY	FREE SPACE	CONFER	LURCHING
REVERBERATED	PRECISELY	MEANDERING	TENDENCY	INTRUSION
EMANATE	AUREOLE	WARY	LAPEL	CONTRADICT

Dicey's Song Vocabulary

SYMMETRICAL	INSISTED	CHARISMA	CONFER	TENDENCY
MINSTREL	LINGERED	PRECISELY	REVERBERATED	CONVENIENT
DIMINISHED	CREMATED	FREE SPACE	AUREOLE	INTRUSION
HARRIED	SULKY	EMANATE	RICKETY	MEANDERING
OPTIMISTIC	MANNIKIN	LURCHING	MISCHIEF	LAPEL

Dicey's Song Vocabulary

CONTRADICT	DUMBFOUNDED	WARY	ANTICIPATING	DECEITFULNESS
ENTHUSIASM	LADEN	MINUET	CONGEALED	BALMY
VAGUELY	INTERFERE	FREE SPACE	CHASTENED	LAPEL
MISCHIEF	LURCHING	MANNIKIN	OPTIMISTIC	MEANDERING
RICKETY	EMANATE	SULKY	HARRIED	INTRUSION

Dicey's Song Vocabulary

EMANATE	VAGUELY	CONGEALED	TENDENCY	WARY
BALMY	FLUENTLY	LADEN	DUMBFOUNDED	DECEITFULNESS
CONVENIENT	DIMINISHED	FREE SPACE	MISCHIEF	AUREOLE
MEANDERING	CONTRADICT	PRECISELY	HARRIED	ENTHUSIASM
LURCHING	LAPEL	REVERBERATED	MANNIKIN	MINSTREL

Dicey's Song Vocabulary

TRIUMPHANTLY	INTERFERE	SULKY	RICKETY	INTRUSION
CHARISMA	CONFER	CHASTENED	CREMATED	ANTICIPATING
SYMMETRICAL	INSISTED	FREE SPACE	LINGERED	MINSTREL
MANNIKIN	REVERBERATED	LAPEL	LURCHING	ENTHUSIASM
HARRIED	PRECISELY	CONTRADICT	MEANDERING	AUREOLE

Dicey's Song Vocabulary

BALMY	SYMMETRICAL	RICKETY	SULKY	INSISTED
ANTICIPATING	WARY	CHASTENED	TRIUMPHANTLY	LADEN
ENTHUSIASM	DUMBFOUNDED	FREE SPACE	MISCHIEF	LINGERED
LAPEL	AUREOLE	TENDENCY	INTERFERE	OPTIMISTIC
LURCHING	FLUENTLY	INTRUSION	MINSTREL	MEANDERING

Dicey's Song Vocabulary

DIMINISHED	MINUET	MANNIKIN	HARRIED	EMANATE
PRECISELY	CONGEALED	CONFER	CONVENIENT	CONTRADICT
VAGUELY	CREMATED	FREE SPACE	CHARISMA	MEANDERING
MINSTREL	INTRUSION	FLUENTLY	LURCHING	OPTIMISTIC
INTERFERE	TENDENCY	AUREOLE	LAPEL	LINGERED

Dicey's Song Vocabulary

LAPEL	ENTHUSIASM	LURCHING	CHARISMA	AUREOLE
DUMBFOUNDED	MINSTREL	LINGERED	DECEITFULNESS	INTERFERE
HARRIED	CREMATED	FREE SPACE	MANNIKIN	BALMY
CONGEALED	MEANDERING	TENDENCY	CONTRADICT	MISCHIEF
CONFER	MINUET	CONVENIENT	FLUENTLY	INTRUSION

Dicey's Song Vocabulary

SULKY	CHASTENED	REVERBERATED	ANTICIPATING	OPTIMISTIC
PRECISELY	VAGUELY	SYMMETRICAL	TRIUMPHANTLY	LADEN
WARY	DIMINISHED	FREE SPACE	RICKETY	INTRUSION
FLUENTLY	CONVENIENT	MINUET	CONFER	MISCHIEF
CONTRADICT	TENDENCY	MEANDERING	CONGEALED	BALMY

Dicey's Song Vocabulary

CONVENIENT	INTRUSION	VAGUELY	TENDENCY	REVERBERATED
ANTICIPATING	OPTIMISTIC	BALMY	MINUET	LINGERED
MISCHIEF	ENTHUSIASM	FREE SPACE	CONFER	MINSTREL
EMANATE	WARY	TRIUMPHANTLY	LAPEL	SULKY
CONTRADICT	CHARISMA	CREMATED	LURCHING	CONGEALED

Dicey's Song Vocabulary

DUMBFOUNDED	RICKETY	SYMMETRICAL	AUREOLE	CHASTENED
INSISTED	FLUENTLY	DIMINISHED	MEANDERING	DECEITFULNESS
LADEN	INTERFERE	FREE SPACE	HARRIED	CONGEALED
LURCHING	CREMATED	CHARISMA	CONTRADICT	SULKY
LAPEL	TRIUMPHANTLY	WARY	EMANATE	MINSTREL

Dicey's Song Vocabulary

ANTICIPATING	MINUET	CONTRADICT	LINGERED	INSISTED
PRECISELY	LADEN	HARRIED	DIMINISHED	FLUENTLY
SYMMETRICAL	AUREOLE	FREE SPACE	EMANATE	MANNIKIN
OPTIMISTIC	MISCHIEF	MEANDERING	DUMBFOUNDED	BALMY
INTERFERE	LAPEL	TRIUMPHANTLY	VAGUELY	CREMATED

Dicey's Song Vocabulary

SULKY	REVERBERATED	RICKETY	WARY	CONFER
TENDENCY	INTRUSION	LURCHING	CONGEALED	CHARISMA
CONVENIENT	DECEITFULNESS	FREE SPACE	MINSTREL	CREMATED
VAGUELY	TRIUMPHANTLY	LAPEL	INTERFERE	BALMY
DUMBFOUNDED	MEANDERING	MISCHIEF	OPTIMISTIC	MANNIKIN

Dicey's Song Vocabulary

DIMINISHED	WARY	CHASTENED	SYMMETRICAL	LAPEL
CONGEALED	INTRUSION	DECEITFULNESS	CONVENIENT	TRIUMPHANTLY
ENTHUSIASM	EMANATE	FREE SPACE	TENDENCY	DUMBFOUNDED
INSISTED	SULKY	REVERBERATED	LADEN	HARRIED
OPTIMISTIC	LURCHING	FLUENTLY	ANTICIPATING	AUREOLE

Dicey's Song Vocabulary

RICKETY	INTERFERE	CHARISMA	MEANDERING	MINUET
BALMY	CONFER	MANNIKIN	MINSTREL	LINGERED
CONTRADICT	VAGUELY	FREE SPACE	MISCHIEF	AUREOLE
ANTICIPATING	FLUENTLY	LURCHING	OPTIMISTIC	HARRIED
LADEN	REVERBERATED	SULKY	INSISTED	DUMBFOUNDED

Dicey's Song Vocabulary

SULKY	LADEN	CHARISMA	OPTIMISTIC	SYMMETRICAL
LAPEL	MEANDERING	CONTRADICT	MINSTREL	CONFER
CONGEALED	REVERBERATED	FREE SPACE	MANNIKIN	CONVENIENT
ENTHUSIASM	CHASTENED	BALMY	ANTICIPATING	DUMBFOUNDED
INSISTED	EMANATE	TRIUMPHANTLY	WARY	MISCHIEF

Dicey's Song Vocabulary

VAGUELY	INTERFERE	MINUET	TENDENCY	RICKETY
HARRIED	AUREOLE	DIMINISHED	INTRUSION	LURCHING
FLUENTLY	PRECISELY	FREE SPACE	CREMATED	MISCHIEF
WARY	TRIUMPHANTLY	EMANATE	INSISTED	DUMBFOUNDED
ANTICIPATING	BALMY	CHASTENED	ENTHUSIASM	CONVENIENT

www.ingramcontent.com/pod-product-compliance
Lightning Source LLC
Chambersburg PA
CBHW081456070526
44586CB00019B/2385